HOW
HITS
HAPPEN

HOW
HITS
HAPPEN

FORECASTING PREDICTABILITY
IN A CHAOTIC MARKETPLACE

Winslow Farrell

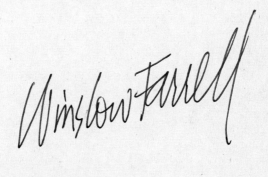

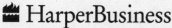 **HarperBusiness**
An Imprint of HarperCollinsPublishers

HarperCollins books may be purchased for educational, business, or sales promotional use. For information please write: Special Markets Department, HarperCollins Publishers Inc., 10 East 53rd Street, New York, NY 10022.

FIRST EDITION

Library of Congress Cataloging-in-Publication Data has been applied for.

ISBN 0-88730978-X

00   01   02   03   04   RRD   10   9   8   7   6   5   4   3   2   1

To my girls

CONTENTS

FOREWORD

Tucked in some recess at the back of our minds is a wishful view of the business world as predictable, plannable, and controllable by our actions. In this imaginary world, new products are spreadsheeted and marketed and launched and go on to achieve their targets according to fixed schedules and budgets.

But such a world may not exist these days. And certainly, as Win Farrell shows us in this book, it bears no resemblance to the realms of fashion, or movies, or publishing, or branded retailing, or toy manufacturing. In these arenas, big-budget launchings can crash, and modest offerings can go into orbit. This is the world of hits and flops.

What makes a movie like *The Full Monty* suddenly take off? Why is it that the first *Star Wars* movie, dismissed originally as a genre potboiler, grew eventually into a cultural phenomenon? Hits build from the ground up, says Farrell. A movie, a new toy, a fashion appears. It has appeal. It touches something inside us, tickles us. The word goes out. Other people get in on it. The word spreads. Suddenly it's a hot ticket. It's more than hot—it's cool. And if the impact is large enough, it even begins to define *cool*. It becomes a phenom. And like *Star Wars* and James Dean and Coke and blue jeans, it may go on to become part of the culture.

What Farrell is writing about here is fashion as a nonlinear phenomenon. And what he does is bring insights from the new sciences of nonlinearity into the world of business. These new sciences are fascinated with "complexity"—with the patterns that form from the simple interactions of individual elements, be they stars in a galaxy, or dipoles in a ferromagnet, or cells in an immune system. Under the influence of the traditional sciences, we have been taught to see business and industry as linear, predictable. A dollar's worth of marketing brings a dollar's worth of reward. But in complexity theory, we abandon our traditional focus on plans and spreadsheets. We become conscious that markets are made up of individual consumers (the stars—or dipoles, or cells—of the economy) who interact with one another and communicate and talk and compare. Collectively their choices begin to define what is desirable. Patterns form. Choices amplify themselves. Hits happen. Unexpectedly, brands appear, compete, lock in, generate cash, disappear. Farrell guides us through this world of business as formation, where markets are processes and brands become self-reinforcing phenomena.

Building products, building brands, is like building fires. A lot of care is needed at the start to see that the initial pieces light the others. There is a critical phase where just a little boosting ensures a subsequent blaze. If the wood is wet, no huffing and puffing can breathe life into the dampness. But these are just the basics. Farrell talks of network externalities, of the benefits to those who latch onto what is becoming prevalent. He talks of the psychology of style, how our style defines us to our peers—and to ourselves. He explores the mechanisms of lock-in, where a single player dominates a market and becomes hard to shift. He describes a computerized model of hits he and his colleagues have built, where miniature "consumers in the machine" (computer programs) observe new launches and one another and try to win social prestige by predicting new waves of fashion better than their neighbors. Fascinating.

In the linear business world, where interactive effects are minimal, executive strategy is simple enough—at least in theory. Keep product moving. Get costs down. Bring quality up. Keep customers happy. In practice, of course, carrying this through is an art. And in nonlinear worlds, things get even more complicated. There is much more to building hits than good design, wonderful content, and timely boosts at takeoff. There is a "metagame," Farrell points out, where managers cannot only take advantage of reinforcing behavior but set up an environment of reinforcing behavior in their favor.

There are issues of release dates and promotion strategies. Promotion itself needs to be determined on the fly, because it depends on how the dynamics shape themselves. Strategy must also consider how expectations form, because products can take off if enough people—and the right people—believe they will take off. Strategists need to determine which people are in a position to influence expectations, just as they must in a presidential primary or other political campaign. The nonlinear world demands excellent products and low costs. But for strategists it offers vastly richer options. And those who learn to play the game well can vastly profit.

What can we learn from Farrell's viewpoint? If we saw our

business, our industry, through his eyes, would it make a difference? I believe so. A few years ago, I was interested in the success of a book that was hovering on and off the scientific bestseller lists. I called the publisher. Had they put together an advertising budget? No, they had not. I told them I believed that the book would take off if they gave it a modest push. If they advertised it, they might have a bestseller on their hands. Good heavens, said the publisher, we are not a cigarette company, are we? The book subsequently faded. I am sure the publisher was a thoughtful man. But he did not understand nonlinearity. He did not understand the dynamics of his industry—the dynamics of just about all industries that sell to consumers who are influenced by other consumers. He needed to read this book.

Win Farrell worked on the Mars Viking Project at the Jet Propulsion Lab in Pasadena. So he is a genuine rocket scientist as well as a business thinker. But rocket science this book is not. It is clear and readable. It is entertaining. And it is the best book I have seen yet on what the new ideas of complexity theory have to do with the concerns of business. Read it and enjoy it. I hope it will be a hit.

—W. BRIAN ARTHUR
Citibank Professor, Santa Fe Institute

ACKNOWLEDGMENTS

This book wouldn't have been remotely possible without the scientific contributions of researchers from the Santa Fe Institute (SFI). I never cease to learn from these colleagues and friends, including Brian Arthur, Chris Langton, Stu Kauffman, David Lane, Scott Page, John Miller, John Casti, Bernardo Huberman, Terry Senjowski, and John Holland. The management staff at SFI have been fabulous—thanks to Ellen Goldberg, Susan Balleti, Marita Prandoni, Andi Sutherland, and everyone. While at SFI, I have met other members of the business community who have gone out of their way to help me apply these ideas to commerce, notably Roger Burkhart and Bill Fulkerson of Deere and Co., Mark Venables of Sainsbury's, Henry Lichstein of Citibank, Dean LeBaron, and Esther Dyson. Thanks to Mike Simmons and Bruce Abell, who suggested I contact the legendary John Hiles and his company Thinking Tools, central to the development of TeleSim.

The support of Coopers & Lybrand Consulting (now PricewaterhouseCoopers) made this book a reality. Thanks to John Jacobs, Dennis Conroy, Andy Zimmerman, Jack Dunleavy, Glen Macdonald, and Terry Umans for their reviews of the manuscript and the support of Michelle DeFranco, Andra

Anzano, Milin Bastidas, and the staff of the Telecom and Media practice. The Emergent Solutions Group at Coopers & Lybrand collectively and individually have a special place in my heart. Many thanks to the perspiration and inspiration behind our efforts to produce the finest software in the world, from Wei Lin, Radek Zapert, George Janes, Wenyu Jing, Bruce Taylor, Iris Ginsberg, Jian Ping Shen, Huanrui Hu, Joe Oh, Grace-Yiying Zhang, Lili Qui, Brandon Weber, Steve Buonocontri, Peter Kowalski, Manor Askenazi, Thor Sigvaldason, Scott DeMarchi, Timothy Heath, Todd Kaplan, Eric Bass, Bernhard Borges, Lyle Scruggs, and Tom Bok. Many thanks for the fantastic research and creative writing from Gerry Caffrey and Mimi Calter. The Treewell portion was largely written by Rob Bernard, who was, as usual, a great devil's advocate in his painstaking reviews of each chapter. The fashion section borrowed heavily from Anita Shieh's fine contributions. A very special thanks to Herbert Godoy for all his help in so many ways, especially in handling the *Anastasia* craze.

Our clients have helped enormously. Many thanks to Simon Bax, Mary Ensminger, and Susan Link of Twentieth Century Fox for believing in us. Also thanks to Mike Shalett and Mike Fine of SoundScan for their support in the early times. A cordial thank-you to Fran Austin and the team at NYNEX and Bob Barada and his team at Pacific Telesis for their support of the genesis of TeleSim. And a warm thank-you to Mike Glinsky, Kevin Smith, and Leroy Williams of USWest and to Bill Archer of AT&T. Thanks to my friend Ric Hendee of Cotton for his contributions—and a big hand to Bill Connell of Macy's for his support.

A special thanks to Doug Kester and to my lifelong friend

Charles Tansey, who have both contributed invaluably to this effort, beginning long before I began writing.

Thanks for the fabulous story of Ernie and Elmo from Baxter Urist of Children's Television Workshop and Neil Friedman, president of Tyco Playschool.

A warm thanks also to Chuck and Belinda Bralver for getting this whole project rolling by introducing me to Adrian Zackheim of HarperBusiness.

And finally, a maximum degree of thanks to Tom Ehrenfeld, who taught me so much about writing and was so instrumental to the development and completion of this book, and a commensurate level of thanks to Laureen Rowland for her patient and motivational role as editor. Many thanks to the promotion staff at HarperCollins, especially Lisa Berkowitz and Amy Lambo.

And thanks to my family for their unwavering support. Hey, Mom! Hey, Dad! We did it! Thanks, Di, Hil, and Marg. This is for you.

INTRODUCTION

The Birth of the Hits Economy

It's now after the turn of the century. Y2K came and went. The hype and apprehension were the big story, not any event itself. Many of us watched ABC's Peter Jennings report on country after country turning the lights on in the new millennium without a hitch. Around the world we went, from New Zealand, to Japan, Russia, Europe, and then the Americas. All the lights on, ATMs at the ready, champagne flowing, Times Square ball dropping. A global view of a world in celebration, not of calamity. In retrospect, we all knew it would go so smoothly, yet months before, contingency plans had been drawn up in company after company. We didn't restrict the banking community in Manhattan from ingress and egress. The visual moment never occurred—CNN had no footage of fistfights breaking out along the queues formed behind the few working ATMs, because our expectations of that massive crisis, swirling up from a few flashpoints, never took place.

Expectations and the apprehensions of widespread computer outages on January first and the social crises that would arise have now receded into the past. The End Is Near signs have been put away, another crisis in our minds, where reality was so much more benign. In the aftermath, we hear stories about winners and losers born of the New Economy, and wonder if there really was a time when that New Economy, whatever it may become, was just getting started.

Perhaps *How Hits Happen* was written at that precise moment in time when things were coming together, and coming apart. Woodstock plus thirty. Baby boomers embracing middle age as Gen-Xers created a even newer world. Hit examples from this era stand timeless and represent a moment when the tectonic plates of old and new economies had begun to part ways, to drift into each other and create vast new mountains of wealth out of their collisions.

These days, it is fashionable in geology to search geophysical records for evidence of craters from asteroid impacts that occurred at the precise moment of epoch change. Utter extinction of the most successful life-form on earth, the trilobites, from an asteroid slamming into Australia. Dinosaurs wiped out from an impact in the Yucatán. Were these meteorite hits the seminal forces behind plate tectonics in geology and did they punctuate evolution in biology? Did they provide the initial energy that drove a stake into the ground, literally, giving rise to the creation of higher intelligence on our planet? Is Silicon Valley the ground zero—the "stake in the ground"— that propelled the creation of the New Economy?

In the years after *How Hits Happen* was written, we have come to expect previously unseen levels of high volatility in the stock market, with day traders flush with cash one day and penniless the next. How much of this volatility is due to the stronger connections we now hold across all of the global capital markets, where contagions sweep across market sectors and slam into new geographies in seconds?

The Spice Girls and their now grandfatherly simian ancestors, the Monkees—so-called manufactured music groups from decades before—are created from a seemingly endless supply of handsome children: 'N Sync, the Backstreet Boys, handpicked like prize livestock into the "best of breeds." Hootie & the Blowfish is now a part of our cultural heritage.

We are each a cog in the biggest hit of them all, the Web. Colossal money-making opportunities arise overnight. Marketing has never before held the promise of being so precise, one-to-one, and in real time. Leaving the privacy issue aside, a vast ocean of consumer data now available from website click-streams can reveal patterns of human behavior never before articulated with such high fidelity.

The realization of the power of market lock-in, made relevant in this new world through the reapplication of the Sherman Anti-Trust Act on Microsoft, has placed put a spotlight on the entire notion of wealth creation from positive feedback forces in the economy.

Hits, created out of human impact, have each made their mark on earth in a new way—and collectively reshaped our economy—into the old and the new. Pokémon, Java, and eBay; at first glance, are three business stories that do not seem to share a common set of laws. Yet their relevance to managers today is critical. Each qualifies as hits: blockbuster products that have emerged from the market and whose success garners a disproportionate share of the public's mind, heart, and wallet. As such they play a starring role in today's economy. Hits more prevalent, more important, and more powerfully felt than ever. It's fair to say that hits-like behavior is becoming a hit in its own right. It's more than the phenomenal madness surrounding Ricky Martin, the manic passion for Furbies during 1999's holiday season, or the national mania for Snoopy dolls that gripped Hong Kong in 1998. A new form of consumer behavior is beginning to define virtually every facet of what could be called the Hit Economy. In the Hit Economy, blockbuster products leverage the aggregated buzz that forms around a product or service into a self-catalyzing force. We're familiar with hits such as *The Blair Witch Project*, which grossed hundreds of millions in worldwide box office receipts; Beanie Babies, which for so long showed no sign of abating as a collectible; or this year's hot teen singer, Christina Aguilera.

When these people and products capture the public fancy, they do so as a seeming fad, driven by a combination of word of mouth, media attention, and carefully stoked marketing messages. Regardless of whether the products are good or not, their success seems fueled primarily by their own success: people are buying because others are buying, and in the collective process they are connecting with one another.

Such laws are no longer limited to Hush Puppies and *Austin Powers*. Hits dynamics underlie the growth of many of the most celebrated companies of the Internet economy. Internet stars such as Amazon.com, eTrade, and other top-tier players lever their high visibility profiles into a self-catalyzing success, using their reputation as highly trafficked areas to draw disproportionately higher crowds. eBay CEO Meg Whitman attributes the explosive success of her company to the "network effect," which *Fortune* magazine calls "an escalating cycle in which sellers attract buyers and vice versa." These new entities create their own storm of self-interest; the more they are used, the more people become locked in to these companies. Such emergent behavior helps the company become the best or even only way of conducting particular forms of commerce.

Consider the behavior of Internet stocks, whose runaway share prices stem from "momentum"—another word for white-hot investor interest. Day traders and other new participants are spending less time and energy focusing on value and more on the relative excitement among buyers and sellers, one that resembles bank runs more than it does traditional stock-picking methods. These stocks leap in value due to the Hit Economy corollary of the efficient market theory, which essentially argues that the price of a stock reflects all the relevant information concerning the stock at the present time. Buzz in today's stock market—and in particular, the ability of a stock to spawn a conversation that forms a community of like-minded buyers—plays a greater role than ever in the rapid surges and declines of hot stocks.

Hits behavior also plays a larger role in the spread of ideas in today's culture. Consider the most significant political story at the end of the century: the near-impeachment of President Clinton for his trysts with Monica Lewinsky. *New Yorker* writer John Cassidy pointed out in an article titled "Monicanomics" that the massive media attention afforded to the presidential intern was a classic example of positive feedback, and as such, was subject to Hits dynamics. The key to successful management in the information business is to recognize which products have the potential to create these network effects—economists call them "network externalities" and promote them as aggressively as possible. This is what Artisan did with *Blair Witch*, it is what CNN did with the Gulf War, and it is what MSNBC did with the Lewinsky story.

Why Hits?

Two profound forces are behind the rise of the Hit Economy. The first is the widespread adoption of the Internet, which has led to the rise of a new set of laws concerning consumer behavior; and the second is the increased digitization of products, enabling their rapid distribution among like-minded consumers.

As the Internet connects more people, compresses time, disassembles markets, and obliterates geography, the ensuing reaggregation of popular culture is characterized more and more by nonlinear results. Unlike the predictable responses businesses could once count on from, say, a direct marketing campaign designed to fuel consumer interest, consumer demand today is surging in waves that are more difficult to predict. As networks of like-minded customers form faster, more often, and from a fundamentally different direction—"bottom up rather than top down"—than ever before, managers can no longer count on manufacturing demand. Rather, they should assess markets as a surfer does the ocean: how can they spot the waves of demand as they arise, and then navigate for the longest ride (until, of course, it is time to catch the next one).

Smart hit makers today see markets as dynamic systems

that can be affected with the appropriate stimulus. This marks a significant evolution from the more static mass markets that arose with mass production. The Model T, for example, was sold to huge undifferentiated pools of consumers who received the same marketing messages as their friends and neighbors, and who purchased the same limited selection of items. Today we have customized, one-to-one markets. Rather than sell one product to many customers, seeking ever more purchasers for single goods, companies take a more dynamic approach to individual buyers in the marketplace. They sell more things to better customers. Using the power of technology to leverage existing relationships, they sell vertically to the same customers, rather than horizontally to more. This has in fact led to network markets, in which companies target individuals who form dynamic networks of like-minded buyers on their own.

This networked economy is subject to what economist Brian Arthur calls "increasing returns." "Increasing returns are the tendency for that which is ahead to get farther ahead, for that which loses advantage to gain further advantage. They are mechanisms of positive feedback that operate within markets, businesses, and industries to reinforce that which gains success or aggrevate that which suffers loss," he writes. Such laws govern the Web, where established sites draw more traffic, thereby increasing their allure. In a recent study, physicist Bernando Huberman of Xerox PARC found that the most popular sites on the Web tend to gain an accelerating advantage over their competitors.

The new field of complexity theory, which looks at how simple interactions in a system become more complex when aggregated over time, helps alert managers in this networked world to become more attentive to how new forms of behavior are emerging. As the world is becoming more interrelated, new affinity groups form quicker, more seamlessly, and in different manners than before. These rapid networks are connecting people to one another more deeply and instantly than ever before. These new communities are emerging organically, unpredictably, and without prompting from city planners or market researchers. These geographically independent consumers are catalyzing into global networks that are more alike in their tastes than they are to people who live near them. These networks of consumers who are closely aligned by their simultaneously similar tastes in fashion or computing or other passions are replacing static demographic segmenting.

A recent *New Yorker* article pointed out the rise of "preference data" over traditional demographic and psychographic data. Rather than market products to consumers based on such static data as age, purchasing power, and geography, companies can now tap into dynamic information to market products to consumers based on their historical preferences, and their behavior.

This calls for what I call natural advice from the synthetic world. At one point, managers will be able to tap into a database of more than 250,000 artificial customers: silicon-based "people" who represent real people and their purchasing preferences in a variety of extremely detailed categories. These agents interact with one another, and influence one another's purchasing decisions. When individual products are plugged into this world, we can gauge market truths from the ground up. The power of synthetic customers to discern how hits happen is growing daily. Ultimately, we will determine the speed and persistence of tsunami of consumer and business interest as these ripples build and cascade over different geographies.

Of course while hits stem from the ubiquity of the Internet, and while we are using increasingly sophisticated tools to discern their patterns, one should never lose sight of their very human quality, how they arise when word of mouth among scattered individuals collects into something more than random buzz. Popular products have always served as a form of connective tissue through which people connect to one another. The rise of the Internet is changing the metabolism of this process, but as long as people connect to one another through the clothes they buy, the songs that they sing, the tchotchkes they collect, and most important, the things they care about, then you will have hits.

1

FADS, FASHIONS, AND FAILURES

For me, there was something deeply intriguing, and
deeply beautiful, about this self-organized emergence of
order from disorder, of complexity from simplicity.

—MITCHELL RESNICK
Turtles, Termites, and Traffic Jams

In December 1994 a small bar band with the unusual name of
Hootie & the Blowfish blipped onto the radar screen of popular
culture. Around the country a few college stations had begun
to play their first single, a catchy song entitled "Hold My
Hand," which soon caught on with alternative stations. Before
long, it began to generate significant radio play on Top 40 stations as well.

And then, seemingly out of nowhere, the band exploded
into the mainstream. Their debut album, *Cracked Rear View*,
soared to the top of the *Billboard* charts. MTV's sister station,
VH1, put their video into heavy rotation. The band went from
an opening act for the hip group Toad the Wet Sprocket to a
headliner in concert halls reserved for top bands like Smashing

Pumpkins or Pearl Jam. They appeared on the cover of *Rolling Stone* and, on one of their three appearances on the David Letterman show, received the cranky host's enthusiastic endorsement. They were not merely successful; they were suddenly stars. After one year on the charts, their debut album had sold more than thirteen million copies, making them one of the fastest-selling bands of all time.

In 1990, the state of Rhode Island's solid stretch of prosperity finally started to slow. Real estate values had risen dramatically over the past decade—a developer's dream. The expanding availability of credit for speculative real estate transactions had helped drive up land values, and the rise in land values had enabled developers to borrow more against their real estate portfolios. Among the most aggressive lenders in this market were some of the state's largest credit unions. Although they were not traditional commercial real estate lenders, they found the prospective profit margins on the speculative real estate transactions simply too attractive to pass up; so attractive, in fact, that even as the market slowed they continued to book loans and expand their deposits aggressively.

But as 1990 came to a close, hints of trouble appeared. Following the publication of a news article about the criminal activities of an official of a bank insured by the Rhode Island Share and Deposit Indemnity Corporation (RISDIC), depositors began quietly removing their deposits from other RISDIC-insured institutions. Most of the credit unions and several banks were insured by RISDIC. Deposits in these institutions had no federal guarantee, and RISDIC had only $25 million to backstop their $1.5 billion in deposits. At one of the most aggressive of the lenders, the approximately $300-million Rhode Island Central Credit Union, withdrawals were particularly large. Several newspaper reporters picked up on this and reported the nervous behavior. At first, the daily total was less than $1 million, but as the story grew and more and more people became aware of the withdrawals and followed suit, that number grew. By December 31, 1990, withdrawals at Rhode Island Central reached $7 million. The next day, the new governor was forced to declare a banking emergency and proceeded to close the forty-five credit unions and banks that had been insured by RISDIC.

Of the forty-five closed institutions, thirty-two were soon able to reopen with federal insurance, merge, or otherwise pay off their depositors. The remaining thirteen institutions, with approximately $1.2 billion in deposits, remained closed, preventing an estimated one third of Rhode Islanders from access to their money. It was the worst financial crisis in the state's history.

Fast-forward to the current long-distance wars. AT&T, which once held a market share of 100 percent, has, since its breakup, seen its share in its core residential market erode to less than 70 percent. Over the past fifteen years, competitors have not merely stolen Ma Bell's market share but fundamentally changed the rules of the game. What was once a premium branded service has become a commodity. And what was once a guaranteed customer base is now a cutthroat competition complicated by competitive rates, incentive promotions, and celebrity spokespeople.

One may not be able to think of a more chaotic business than recorded music, a messy world of wild, creative artists and constantly changing tastes. As Chris Rock says about its pace of change: *here today, gone today*. We expect people to buy music with their gut; what we don't anticipate is predictability. Veterans of the industry may have acquired an intuitive feel for the market, but no one expects that they can manufacture blockbusters on demand. Hits in this world appear to come out of the blue.

In Rhode Island, likewise, no one could have foretold that the system was preparing to shift. Nor could one know whether the shift itself would be slow and gradual or fast and precipitous. In retrospect, onlookers might have seen that shifts in lending moods indicated that the system was headed for a dangerous fall. And yet those same signs (e.g., asset growth profitability) could also have been read as indicators of greater prosperity in the near future. Lenders and regulators admit they lack the innate knowledge to predict how and when the system will end in a free fall. They long for a tool that could be trusted to forecast when they are headed for trouble, a tool to guide their decision making.

Finally, with AT&T, it seems remote that management could have known that a change in consumer behavior was likely. Once the company began to lose market share, customers seemed to flee to competitors at a desperate pace. The old way of doing business crumbled, and there was no ready replacement on the shelf. What the company needed was a way to pick up on the change in the market's mood, and a model that showed how this shifting mood might play out in consumer behavior.

These three examples, which span a continuum of seemingly stable worlds, show that in business everywhere, we are increasingly confronting situations that defy simple explanation. It's no revelation that the world of recorded music has always been unpredictable. Lending in commercial real estate, on the other hand, has always been considered cyclical: there's a long-established pattern that purportedly dictates that "what goes up always comes down." Yet at any one point in time, no single expert can say definitively where we are in the cycle, or how to get out before the other guy. Even a seemingly stable market like long-distance phone service can undergo industry-altering change that overthrows and rewrites the rules of the game. No one today is immune to market changes that appear to be sudden, multifaceted, and inscrutable.

So, how does one respond? Typically people react to these scenarios by seeking simple answers. As managers and leaders, we prefer multiple choice to essay questions and true/false questions to anything else. Rather than analyze problems in their true multifaceted dimension, managers construct myths about cause and effect. They try to forecast the future by relying upon past performance and a traditionally linear vision of spreadsheets. If a business unit increased its revenues by 15 percent over the last three years, managers tell themselves, they project the next three years' performance by simply multiplying by 1.15. Others turn to consultants for help, believing that only they can distill the simple truth from the bubbling crude of complex ooze, or that like wizards, they will look into the future and magically make the unknowable transparent.

Each of these attempts is doomed to fail. Why? In each of these cases, the simple answers to "why" may never be precisely determined. That's because there are no smoking guns or easy answers. Rather, one must look at the world—and at consumers—in a manner that accommodates and in fact embraces its complex and constantly shifting nature. One must give up the search for simplicity and begin to look at business in a radical new way: though the lens of *complexity*.

Beyond Simplicity

Complexity theory is a way of looking at the world that begins to give shape and meaning to seemingly inexplicable and unrelated scenarios. This perspective helps explain everything from how hurricanes form to how fads explode into the public's imagination. It helps address such questions as why stock markets crash or why traffic jams form. It explores the forces behind the breakup of the Soviet Union. Complexity theory even addresses such questions as how matter eventually clumped together to form sentient beings.

Complexity theory is a nascent field of scientific study that is just starting to gain notice in the public eye. Over the past two decades a growing number of thinkers have been developing a body of work that seeks to explain how large systems emerge, adapt, and eventually produce results. Everything

from natural evolution to emerging forms of political gover-
nance has been put under the complexity microscope.

Complexity theory draws from and reflects a postmodern
view of the world. It is based on quantum physics and existen-
tialist philosophy rather than Newtonian physics and Cartesian
thought. Rather than analyze and break the world apart through
a linear, top-down, mechanistic point of view—as we usually
do—complexity theory rests on decentralization and nonlinear
events. Randomness and chaos are not rejected but embraced.

This school of thinking was launched by noted physicist
and Nobel laureate Philip W. Anderson and a group of his colleagues, an eclectic bunch of economists, biologists, mathe-
maticians, and other thinkers who established the Santa Fe
Institute in the foothills of Santa Fe, New Mexico, in 1984. The
group, which includes such famous scientists as Nobel laureate
Murray Gell-Mann and MacArthur fellow Stuart Kauffman, has
produced a growing body of work about complexity that has
helped provide insights into everything from the way the
body's immune system fights disease to how Microsoft has
come to dominate the market of computer operating systems.

In my work at Coopers & Lybrand (now Pricewaterhouse-
Coopers) we have begun to apply some of these principles to
business systems. But make no mistake—this book is not an
attempt to break new scientific ground. Many great thinkers
with scientific credentials have already plowed the field. With
this book I hope to open the eyes of businesspeople everywhere to the world of synthetic customers, a world of consumers who behave as unpredictably as real people, and show
how these artificial worlds can revolutionize the way we look
at the behavior of real consumers like you or me. Specifically, I

hope to show how even a basic understanding of the principles of complexity can in fact become an invaluable tool for managers and leaders in any organization in any industry.

Over the past five years, I have been working to bring these principles to a broad range of clients. I have helped telecommunications companies plan the most effective strategy for launching new services, movie executives decide the most effective marketing campaign for a film, and retailers assess how best to staff a store floor so as to maximize their resources and appeal to the ever-quirky consumer. Now I hope to help others in business by presenting the basic tenets of complexity in a clear, accessible way so that you too can make better sense of today's chaotic marketplace.

This ambition, in fact, ties into a central foundation of complexity theory—that *making sense is the most powerful form of action*. Managers faced with complex systems can't achieve their objectives by making static projections or assuming a fixed set of beliefs. Nor can they optimize their businesses simply by cranking up the volume—that is, by installing more powerful chips, hiring more workers, yelling louder, working harder. Given the fast-changing and ever-increasingly complex nature of the world, gaining insight into how patterns are forming and structures are developing represents the most powerful way of managing in the new economy.

Hidden Order

So just what is complexity?

Complexity is the study of *complex adaptive systems*: large systems comprised of a great many agents that interact with one another in a great many ways. Economies comprise an enormous number of people and firms engaged in various transactions, for example, just as the brain consists of innumerable neurons that are interconnected. Other systems include ecologies, immune systems, or developing embryos.

These complex systems contain such a huge number of interactions that they defy simple principles. Santa Fe scientist Chris Langton has said that complex systems operate "on the edge of chaos and order." That is, these systems are neither orderly, in which simple agents operate under predictable laws, nor are they chaotic, in which matter operates in a predictably unpredictable way. Rather, over time, rules and principles about how the players in the system interact emerge from their behavior. They do not conform to a fixed set of rules emanating from a single source. Instead there is what some scientists have called a "hidden order" that organizes the system's ever-changing dynamics.

Complexity represents an attempt to identify how new rules emerge from the interactions of the particles in the system. As the parts interact, they undergo spontaneous self-organization. In an economy, for instance, people satisfy their needs and desires, which can be organized into buying patterns. An embryo begins to take shape from a cluster of DNA. In a flock of birds there is always one bird that leads, but no one bird is the leader. Rather, as the flock flies, different birds assume the front position over time, taking the lead as the spot opens up. A standing ovation is another example of an emergent phenomenon, socially constructed by the independent actions of individuals. Such decentralized systems, with their own self-organizing properties, are the essence of complex adaptive systems.

Much of the work at the Santa Fe Institute relies upon the use of extremely powerful computers that create simulations of complex adaptive systems. With their ability to process billions of interactions that build upon one another in an adaptive manner, computer worlds help researchers gather insight into the "real" world. By sending agents into artificial worlds we can achieve insights somewhat akin to the perspective space scientists gain by sending probes to other planets.

At PricewaterhouseCoopers Emergent Solutions Group (ESG), which I lead, we have developed a software program composed of more than 250,000 synthetic consumers—artificial agents who are endowed with both objective and subjective attributes. Each consumer is identified by his or her demographics (age, income, address) and psychographics— the agents have the ability to form friendships, spread gossip about hot new products, have opinions, and quickly change them about new products. We can plug in a product like the new Britney Spears release or a Pokémon toy and, in essence, test their hit quality. The patterns of interaction among the agents, in turn, provide guidance as to how companies can successfully launch hit products.

Discovering Complexity

As someone who has worked both as a consultant and as a computer expert, I have found in complexity theory a way of looking at the world that addresses real and virtual problems as they actually are.

My discovery of this new science came in the midst of a languishing reengineering engagement in 1992. Dennis Conroy, who at the time headed up Coopers & Lybrand's consulting group for the telecommunications industry, needed a radically new way of thinking about how to reorganize a client of ours, a local telephone exchange company. Conventional wisdom steered us toward "bigger is better"—we should treat this company like a factory, with standardized outputs and production systems that would wring out all unnecessary costs.

Dennis had a different approach. He asked me to help him build up the arguments for a "small is beautiful" design: One functional organization would be broken into myriad small, virtually stand-alone telephone companies. Although they would be united through common systems and languages of network design, they would also be different in a fundamental way that would grow out of their own local geographies. Most important, each company would be guided by its own singular competitive ecology.

Dennis and Andy Zimmerman (another partner in the group at the time) convinced the firm that we should invest in developing a different approach to building organizations for a rapidly changing landscape. I got the charge. My background was in visual presentations of complicated concepts, so naturally I first mapped out the competitive ecology of the telecom landscape on paper. But as I researched this project, instead of drawing from books that illustrated ideas and concepts about the latest advances in machine intelligence, computer architectures, and programming languages, I found myself looking at volumes on the latest thinking in biology and ecology. I became fascinated with the representations of large-scale ecological systems and the linkages among dispersed elements found in the biosphere.

There seemed to be a unifying mill of ideas about how competition would evolve over time in a technologically driven, human setting. But I wasn't seeing it yet. That night, at a winter holiday party in my hometown of Westport, Connecticut, I was distracted by these thoughts. Individuals shaped an ecological community that could remain somewhat stable until altered by the introduction of a foreign species, just as Hawaii's ecosystem had been damaged by the onslaught of nonindigenous species of insects, flora, and birds. But how could one gain insight into how these linkages interacted?

That night, serendipity struck. As I settled into bed and flipped through a recent copy of *Scientific American*, I found what I was looking for. I read about three scientists who were working on different aspects of a new set of scientific inquiries: W. Brian Arthur, who was studying the increasing-returns economics that appears to dominate technology-centered industries; Stuart Kauffman, who was building a model of how life formed from the universe; and Chris Langton, who had built a new science in "artificial life," the name given to a new discipline that studies "natural" life by attempting to re-create biological phenomena from scratch within computers and other "artificial" media. As I read this article I became more and more convinced that these three had been working on the same problems that I was trying to solve. I became at once more agitated and intrigued.

The following Monday I explained to my colleagues at Coopers that I had stumbled upon something really big. I called Stanford University, and to my surprise, reached Brian Arthur, who was an economics professor there. I flew out to the Santa Fe Institute the following week, and soon found myself talking with Chris Langton and Mike Simmons—two of Santa Fe's more renowned experts—about my search. I was trying to determine the appropriate organizational design for a company undergoing transformation from a regulated, glacially evolving environment to one that was going to face brutal competitive threats.

Within moments, Chris was at the board, drawing diagrams that explained the crucial relationship between pheromone trails and the growth of anthills by the coordinated but autonomous actions of ants that followed these reinforced pathways. These colonies were built without architects, from the bottom up, and were intricately attuned to the local ecological conditions.

This viewpoint put everything in perspective. I proposed drawing from their work to create a computer simulation that would portray the changing evolutionary landscape to my client. Mike Simmons agreed with his colleagues and said that without a doubt, computer simulation was the answer. But, he sheepishly admitted, "We've never built one that portrayed businesses. Anthills, yes, but commercial enterprises, no." In that moment I saw tremendous opportunity.

This excitement only heated up the following week, when Brian Arthur met me in his office in the economics department at Stanford. While we sipped coffee, Brian explained how the most effective organizational design came from guerrilla armies, who had at most two layers of supervision over their ground troops. This was a far simpler system than that of the multilayered former Bell system, where vice presidents were known as "fifth levels." I was unsure if I could instantly apply this metaphor to my client's situation, but wanted to salt the idea away and get into even more interesting topics.

We soon settled into a discussion about the importance of increasing returns in telecommunications. The circumstances and motivations were very similar to the technology-based industries such as microcomputer chips and videotape recorders that Brian had been studying. In explaining how these industries worked, Brian's favorite analogy was surfing. Learning to spot and catch the right waves is the mark of a veteran surfer, and, as Brian explained, it is also the mark of a company that enjoys a "first-mover advantage" in business. An ocean wave or a technology-choice demand wave has to be actively surfed with a continuous stream of small but crucial tactical moves. In business, waves of demand must be actively surfed, with an acute knowledge of whether the wave is building up or moving into churning, energy-wasting white water. The essence of a good ride is knowing when to get in and out, and maximizing one's advantage along the way.

Brian agreed with the other members of the Santa Fe Institute that a business simulation was critical to explain the importance of increasing returns and complex adaptive systems. In fact, Brian and his associates John Holland, Richard Palmer, and Blake LeBaron, among others, had already created a computer-simulated stock market. This computer-based market exhibited complex behavior complete with booms and crashes. Its population of simulated traders each operated by a simple set of rules as to how they expected the market to yield a profitable return.

This compelling model offered a greater application for the real world: modeling and forecasting the behavior of companies and the "survival of the fittest" strategies. Since strategies seem to be composed of an intersecting and evolving set of rules, some of which we may not know, or ever write down, we learn to model how our human-derived strategies change under environmental stresses ranging from minor to extreme. We could see whether an existing set of rules was robust enough to withstand difficult times.

Telecom companies, for example, had developed a set of rules about how to behave in a marketplace free of competition. Now, after decades, they were facing competition born of a totally different mind-set—similar to stock market traders with different belief systems about the expectations of value and profit-making opportunities. Would these new competitors be in for the long haul, or would they try to maximize their short-term opportunities? How would the incumbents respond? And how, then, would the stability of the market change, and new rules emerge?

We have become comfortable with this form of behavior in the natural world. After all, magnetism results from lining up the spins of a huge number of iron atoms. In telecom-industry evolution, the environment would be built as a result of feedback from individual strategic choices about product availability and prices, and the market prices' feedback to the individuals making those choices.

With computer simulations, we had the opportunity to test the relationships among these individual choices and aggregated outcome in the artificial market. If we could build a rich enough simulation, managers could try out various strategies and witness the various outcomes. The trials could be numerous and nonthreatening. But the artificial stock market dealt only with a simulated stock. How these simulations might behave when built up from real data, with simulated economic conditions of the various actual players in the real market, was the challenge we faced as we built the first simulation of the telecom marketplace.

This first step held much promise for my work. After working in the rapidly evolving telecom market as a consultant for a decade, I saw that clients often asked for the "most likely" scenario to be played out in time. They wanted to be given "the answer"; where *the* indicated the single right answer, one that would coalesce many years in the future.

The problem with that mind-set was that the telecom market was dynamic. Rapid change took place over the course of weeks, not years, and evolved in utterly unpredictable ways. The discrepancy between the various plausible paths of evolution that the market was taking seemed almost laughably varied. While at every increment you could see how different scenarios might play out, when you projected two different outcomes to their logical extreme it was hard to believe that they stemmed from the same set of facts.

Our markets operated under the principles of self-organization and emergent behavior. I came to see that there was no "most likely" outcome but myriad different possibilities. And that the ultimate winners or losers would be affected by small, chance events at the beginning that would lead the whole market toward one outcome or another. The ultimate winners and losers could wind up on different sides of the tally sheet due to small, seemingly random events that took on added power because they took place during times of great change.

To help executives learn how to cope with change and surprise, we worked alongside John Hiles at Thinking Tools to develop a computer software simulation called TeleSim as a telecom-executive training tool. Yet our early models lacked sufficient "realism" to portray the physics of this bustling world. We found that we needed to take a page from children's video games such as the Nintendo 64 water-racer game, where the water is rendered in such a way that it feels wet and deep.

To help executives with actual decision support, the tool needed to incorporate *all* the physics of their world: real data that captured all the salient information about their market-place. We designed a program with hundreds of thousands of synthetic customers, each endowed with lifelike attributes such as the ability to make decisions, change their minds, and act unpredictably. Only by setting them in motion with one another could we begin to foresee how real potential outcomes might emerge.

These agents were informed by the principles of com-plexity—a model I then had to explain to clients. Many wanted simple football analogies for the new rules at play; the closest I could come up with was a bicycle race in which the main group of bicycles allows drafting by individuals (who encounter less wind when they follow behind the leaders), as an example of cooperative and competitive behavior. The dynamics in a race would be punctuated by periods of relative stasis and individual pursuits, and the eventual winner would be determined by the interaction among the individual competitors during the race.

As I learned about complexity, I saw that we could develop a decision-support tool that would aim at defining consumer demand—one that would not only work for those businesses that had a nearly constant demand level, but would also aim at forecasting the outcome of problems that appeared unsolvable. The most intriguing of these were the best and most difficult targets: "hit" businesses. Perceived as fads, the products of these industries are shaped by dynamic forces. Popular products experience an exponential takeoff rate of sales, one that evolves from the self-organizing properties of word of mouth as demand accelerates.

We figured that if we could begin to develop information that would determine a bit of the physics around fads—around the speed of transmission of word of mouth, for instance— then we could certainly apply this model to all businesses.

Over time our experience of modeling fads and fashions in the would-be worlds of synthetic consumers, along with testing these insights with clients, has revealed three key principles: (1) Time matters. (2) More is different. (3) Learning is living.

Time Matters

In complex systems, time acts as a context that determines the future. That is, the multiple future histories are connected to one single present that acts as the boundary for future events. Over time, history creates "grooved pathways" that reinforce behavior. This may make it more likely that, say, certain products will succeed in the marketplace, regardless of their relative quality.

Consider the Beta format for videocassettes. Why should VHS be the standard for tapes today? No one would argue that it is a technologically superior product. Rather, at the critical time that a standard was forming around which tape to use—and which videocassette player to produce—a number of Japanese manufacturers found the leverage point to tilt the playing field toward VHS. Sony Corporation, which developed Beta and was first to market it, could have used its toehold to persuade other manufacturers to adopt the standard, thus locking in its success. Yet it failed to convince others to support Beta, and thus, over time, consumers chose VHS, which was more readily available.

The arrow of time is singular, but there are a number of adjacently possible histories yet to be written. It is expected that in these near futures, or most of them, VHS videotapes will continue to remain plentiful. DVD may have become the new standard, but only when its promise becomes so evident that a significant number of consumers decide to switch. For other new technologies, such as Internet browsers, Microsoft has taken the market from Netscape. But remember Mosaic? The once-breakthrough browser lies discarded in a historical context; once sought after, Mosaic is now relegated to a receding niche position in the competitively dynamic world of Web browsers. Without a significant base of users any longer, there is no more economic incentive to invest in upgrading the product.

One of Brian Arthur's most powerful contributions to economics and to business strategy is his deep exploration of the principle of increasing returns. Contrary to the traditional economic notion of diminishing returns, whereby additional investment or input yields less output over time, he posits that many systems actually display positive feedbacks. Arthur's theory contrasts with economist Alfred Marshall's view of the industrial world, where firms that gain an advantage eventually run into limitations. Predictable equilibriums in the form of lowering prices are eventually reached in this world. Arthur proposes an alternative in which these equilibriums are fleeting, and never reached.

In this world, success accrues to the successful; market share begets market share. An initial investment in, say, an operating system by Microsoft realizes increasing returns over time. Or, the success of a popular band hits a level where its buzz alone—never mind the inherent quality of its music—accounts for its huge popularity. Consider Hootie & the Blowfish. At a certain point, consumers weren't purchasing the record because it corresponded precisely with their musical taste; they were responding to the buzz around the album. The band had achieved an unstoppable critical mass: word of mouth generated higher sales, which compelled radio and television stations and other media to highlight the band; the higher visibility in turn led to more word of mouth. And so success accrued in this reinforcing cycle.

More Is Different

At their core, complex adaptive systems exhibit nonlinear dynamics. That is, at various junctures, one plus one plus one does not equal three. Or, as Philip Anderson has written, "More is different."

Societies aren't built by simply adding up the traits and characteristics of individuals. When you add one more, and another, and so on, societal traits start to emerge. A new entity grows out of the interactions of these individuals, so as the new system adapts, it displays different behaviors and traits.

Likewise, when a group of consumers becomes a market, you can't determine the macro quality of their purchasing taste by simply adding up all their individual preferences. That method cannot explain the rise of grunge music, for instance, which grew organically from its Seattle home into a nation-wide phenomenon. It also doesn't describe how a group of people comes to a decision about which movie they will see together. At some point the interactions between the people becomes the force that changes and aligns their collective desires.

In order to thrive in a market with such dynamics, managers must begin to think about their world organically—that is, they must see their markets as living systems that operate by the laws of physics, as opposed to a machine that operates under simple laws. The important questions to ask are: How are things interacting? What are the developing patterns? And how can they be influenced?

Nonlinear dynamics show up as surprises and unexpected events. They encompass the moment when things change from the predictable into the unknowable—when something happens to create a fundamentally new set of behaviors.

For example, the *Billboard* chart position of a recorded music single results from recent sales, above a threshold. When a single achieves a certain position—say in the Top 40—the song goes into rotation on a much greater number of radio stations. It then begins to achieve a critical mass of listeners who cause an acceleration of sales. Simply crossing the border from 41 to 40 gives it a significant lift over other singles that are competing on the merits of the musical value, the reputation of the artist, and the level of promotion, among other factors.

Discovering these patterns of nonlinearity and how they shape business lies at the heart of applying complexity theory to managing and marketing. These nonlinear dynamics can be ignored—or embraced. Failing to develop a radar for these changes will ensure an inevitable decline in business as market dynamics change. Learning to spot these patterns gives managers a tool for creating and sustaining hits in the long run.

Learning Is Living

Over time, as systems such as markets and environments change, the agents within them—such as consumers or biological organisms—adapt. In contrast to logical thinking, this trend has more to do with inference and pattern recognition. That is, we make sense of things by connecting the dots.

Often when I am feeling lucky, I will adapt my behavior more instinctively than logically. If I find myself at Foxwoods, a nearby casino, I might move from playing a certain one-armed bandit to another because I win a jackpot and enjoy the reward of those coins. I might stay longer once I begin to lose again because I anticipate that my big payoff is right around the corner. Similarly, in a technology bet like the various forms of digital subscriber line (DSL), the means for transmitting the Internet over local telephone lines, any particular bet may yield a huge payoff, but that remains to be seen. The DSL slot machine still gathers quarters and quarters of additional incremental investment, and we humans wait for the reward.

Programmers at the MIT media lab have built a robot that can react to human movements and actions. Rather than try to endow the robot with knowledge and reasoning, the programmers gave it fast reactive behavior. The robot is adaptive, thus lifelike. The purpose of this robot is to provide entertainment only, but the applications are vast, from movies to amusement park rides. The robot doesn't take the time to develop an optimal approach to reacting to human contact. It learns to adapt.

Most businesses start out simple and inevitably become more complicated over time. If we can find some rules that may govern that bumpy road from simplicity to complexity, we could make more sense out of a business, not just in how it runs, but in how it is likely to change in the future. We could use this understanding to begin to identify, for example, when a business seems headed down an evolutionary path that locks it into an optimal strategic position.

When a business such as a telecom company becomes complicated, and its people need to respond rapidly to a competitive threat—such as an unforeseen price discount offered by a well-capitalized new entrant—managers may rely more on gut instinct than on logical models to effect change. We might expect AT&T to have a strategy similar to that of MCI, but, indeed, AT&T's strategy reflects its heritage and thus more closely resembles the instincts of the Regional Bell Operating

Companies (RBOCs). When the Bell System broke up into eight newly independent companies (AT&T and seven RBOCs), the new companies initially followed related strategic pathways, guided by historical local constraints and market conditions, regulatory constraints, and customer loyalty. Interestingly, as time passes, those strategies evolve—and diverge.

Complexity in Our World

Each of the three examples described at the beginning of this chapter demonstrate how time matters, more is different, and learning is living. In the case of Hootie & the Blowfish, we gathered finely grained data about the rate of sales from SoundScan and recognized some of the patterns by which this group became such a phenomenon.

In our model of how a musical CD becomes a hit, an early group of risk-taking music lovers often tests out new songs and then spreads the word to friends. They do so not merely to share the music but to enhance their social standing: picking a hot new group before it becomes popular gives the early tester a sense of "prognosticator pride" and makes him feel cool around his friends. In the case of Hootie, these early evangelists found the music so appealing that they rushed to tell others, sensing that the group's first CD would sell so well that friends would be impressed with the accuracy and clairvoyance of their early predictions. They in turn created a growing legion of followers who also believed that the CD would become a big hit, and who in turn enjoyed popularity from the positive response to this early, eventually fulfilled prediction.

Witness the spread of an information contagion, where ideas are transmitted like an epidemic. In this outbreak, the words and enthusiasm from these evangelists can be infectious. Like a bee colony sharing information, these ideas, or memes, spread from one person to another, in the process crowding out other, similar ideas. The first to build up a sufficiently loose following can drown out others. In the case of Hootie, for instance, there were perhaps other artists who were arguably more talented whose CDs were unfortunately released at the same time. Yet by dint of being first with their pop melodies and easy beat, the band occupied the top slot for the music industry's equivalent of forever.

The first Hootie evangelists were southern club audiences that fanatically attended shows, spread the word to their friends that a Hootie show was a great evening's entertainment, and spent the money to purchase some of Hootie's homemade CDs. With the later catalyst of airplay and commercial introduction, these early converts became a ready army who spread the word that Hootie was a band whose music would touch millions.

Waves of purchasing begin with the microbursts of interaction from these evangelists, and then catch on with increasing numbers of followers who respect the opinions of these risk-taking initiators. Demand isn't shaped by a single set of adopters, followers, and laggards. Instead, demand is constructed from the bottom up, and waves of demand, plotted over time, accumulate to produce the macro phenomena of a market.

With Hootie & the Blowfish, the bursts of demand that exploded with every concert and club date represent the first signs that a major hit was forming. Over time, by examining the SoundScan data and plugging the Hootie CD into a simulated market, we can see these waves of demand coalesce and shape a throbbing nationwide demand for their first CD as their singles gained airplay and started climbing the charts. It's possible that one single triggered a hunger for the album. But more likely, the growing popularity of the band reinforced consumer belief that Hootie was producing a great sound that made people feel safe about buying, which led to more sales.

We see that waves of demand and popularity grow dramatically after the release of hit singles, such as "Time," released in the fall of 1995. The continual onslaught of sales, week in and week out, following that release brought *Cracked Rear View* its lasting place as one of the most popular albums to date.

The tale of Hootie & the Blowfish is a historic one, a literal groove in a record that blazed a new trail. Hootie was a hit, a novel sound, with a loyal and vocal following, who collectively levered this response to gain an increasing return to its initial club dates. Hootie enjoyed the physics of the hit. These individuals took the form of southern water vapor that eventually took the country by storm.

Sudden Storms

Another storm appeared over Narragansett Bay in 1990, and like a squall, came up suddenly, without warning, and ripped the sails out of long-standing conservative institutions. In hindsight, they should have known better. But they were all so busy trying to outdo one another that they didn't notice that this squall could knock them all onto the rocky shoals.

In Rhode Island, decisions to invest, to grant construction loans, and to regulate lending institutions' criteria produced a sense of value in the burgeoning real estate market. In this interrelated system of property values, bank lending criteria, and wealth, the rising tide of the market reinforced each individual's belief that prices would rise forever, and produced a snowballing effect of property value in the market. As even skeptics saw the market rising, and rising, they too were persuaded to eventually leap into the market, leading finally to a collective and self-reinforcing belief structure in which all the parties became convinced that more and more commercial structures would find ready and willing buyers and renters. Lenders and investors began to base the value of real estate not on the logical and projectable cash-flow streams but on properties that were "comparable" in this overheating market.

The relationship among these different actors was complex, the networks that tied them to one another were many and varied, and the promise of rewards was seductive. That it would end with angry mobs storming the majestic alabaster capitol, with its glittering dome reflecting the signs of bankrupted citizens and its halls echoing the anguished cries of savings account holders pleading for their money, was a far cry from the promise that real estate had held. The networks among these individuals allowed a self-reinforcement of the myth that all would be well, or even better than that.

AT&T demonstrated that long-standing myths about how businesses and industries are supposed to work can be rocked from their foundations by new market competitors who think and behave differently. For the long-distance-telephone-service companies, the issue was not how to win at the existing game but to determine how the game that's being played works—and how to change the rules without the other players knowing that the rules were being changed or that they were losing. Developing new metagames, above the level of the existing struggle for long-distance customers who purchased on the basis of price of a commoditized service, was the challenge faced by MCI, Sprint, and AT&T.

Some incumbent telecom companies have prepared for voice-telephone land wars, only to be invaded by amphibious assault from data and Internet services by no-name start-ups. The most dangerous of these new entrants are those whose actions are nearly random, whose dodges and feints cannot be easily discerned from thrusts and parries. The new entrants that learn from their early successes and quickly adapt their strategies to respond to unexpected avenues of opportunity might be difficult to predict from the incumbent's standpoint, which considers only a limited but long-standing perspective on the "right thing to do."

Niche players can be tolerated for only so long. Incumbents may be loath to drop prices uniformly for a wide number of customer groups in response to a niche player's cut-rate pricing. But unexpected behaviors can also result from the ongoing generation of coupons and rewards to residential customers who switch their supplier. As long as the niche-based company is not large enough to really threaten, then coexistence is encouraged. But once these renegades gain a sufficient degree of market penetration—say 30 percent—then the large players will certainly shift strategies from tolerance to all-out war.

For these three test cases, and for many more examples in

our daily lives as managers and consumers, a model of the market is available, one that helps us begin to understand just how the players in the market might respond to certain factors, especially in times of crisis, speculation, or rapid growth. Based on the principles of complexity, such a model can enable decision makers to understand more fully the psychological factors at play in the development of fads in music, the dynamics of speculative investing, and even the rules that underlie the "logic" of industry structure. This tool helps provide key insights—not just by enabling music executives to lever a hit single into a hot-selling album, or set off warning lights to lending institutions, or show a telecom executive how new rules of competition are evolving. This tool can help managers in all industries find the emerging patterns in their marketplace, take high-leverage actions, and then surf the waves of demand in their market. This perspective helps them find the hidden order in their chaotic world, and use it to their advantage.

2

ANATOMY OF A HIT

A new generation of Americans was breaking away from the habits of its parents and defining itself by its music. There was nothing the parents could do: This new generation was armed with both money and the new inexpensive appliances with which to listen to it. This was the new, wealthier America. . . . But now, as the new middle class emerged in the country, it was creating as a byproduct a brand-new consuming class: the young. . . . The young formed their own community. For the first time in American life they were becoming a separate, defined part of the culture: As they had money, they were a market, and as they were a market they were listened to and catered to. Elvis was the first beneficiary.

By 1956 he had become both a national celebrity and a national issue. His success, amplified as it was by the newfound wealth of the nation and the new technology of radio, record players and finally, television, defied the imagination. He quickly made a three-picture deal with Hal Wallis for $450,000. "Hound Dog" sold 2 million copies and "Don't Be Cruel" sold 3 million. His singles were not merely taking off, they were defying traditional musical categories: "Heartbreak Hotel" was number one on the white chart, number one on the country chart, and number five on the rhythm and blues chart;

"Don't Be Cruel" and "Hound Dog" became number one on all three charts. In April 1956 he already had six of RCA's all-time Top 25 records and he was selling $75,000 worth of records a day.

—David Halberstam,
The Fifties

Hits happen everywhere.

Not just on the fashion runway or in the box-office numbers of Hollywood blockbusters. Hits as we know them signify explosions of demand and happen in every industry today. We have all witnessed these explosions. A white sale at Macy's, for example, is comprised of a series of hits. When this retailer moves the goods on a huge scale it experiences flurries of transactions within the store; the queues that form at the cosmetics or housewares registers constitute small pops in demand. Sometimes hits happen lightning-fast, as in the case of the Harry Potter series. And sometimes hits emerge after a long process. The fax machine, for example, is based on technology that has existed for over one hundred years, yet only exploded into widespread use ten years ago. Explosions take place not just in what we typically consider hits-driven industries like perfume, toys, television, and new hits businesses like video games and Internet sites; they happen everywhere.

Understanding how these patterns emerge and self-organize lies at the heart of understanding hits as products of complex adaptive systems. From Elvis to Tickle Me Elmo, there is an underlying set of dynamics among these hits, a physics of how they begin, evolve, grow, and decay. Managers who become versed in this science will have a powerful tool for launching hits of their own.

These principles are relevant to hits in every industry—from automobiles to pharmaceuticals to websites. In all these areas it's important to learn about what gets the explosion started, how that explosion is kept alive, how many explosions you can expect in certain environments and when.

Hits as Explosions

Because hits emerge as a function of the conversation started around a product or idea, it is essential to look at how people relate to products, and to each other through them. Word of mouth and other social transactions act as the medium through which agents connect, self-organize, and build—much like the acetylcholine by which nerve impulses are transmitted in the brain.

Ever since we first began making the conscious decision to purchase things, businesspeople have been studying why we buy. But until now, studies on marketing have focused on the process as a static one: what makes one person, or many people, prefer one brand of, say, soup to another. Complexity, which sheds light on the dynamics of a system—the way in which many decisions are interrelated and influence one another—provides a new way of understanding how hits happen. By looking at how consumers make their decisions in an interrelated way, and seeing how clusters of buyers form around a product or service in a nonlinear way, complexity offers a new way of seeing what causes one product to leap out of the crowded marketplace and earn a lasting place.

Hits are composed of a great number of people coming to the same frame of mind somewhat simultaneously, without any one force coordinating them. But of course, no one person could wish this like-mindedness into existence. Rather, hits create their own combustion. When enough people get excited about a product, their transactions and conversations ignite the spread of the hit. In such a manner these explosions are built from the bottom up through the aggregation of myriad vibrations: jostling people bumping into one another, one-on-one conversations, individual people paying attention to clever or memorable ads. As patterns of people interacting emerge, their collective behavior goes through nonlinear leaps where the properties change fundamentally, like a mass of proteins that comes to form a living body.

Hits seem as if they happen spontaneously. Yet much like the explosion of a bomb or any other catalytic explosion, hits result from an aggregation of interactions that begins at a basic level and builds until a critical mass explodes into public consciousness. Whether this process is that of networks forming, patterns emerging, or chain reactions taking place, all begin with a single event and build to the larger process.

This interaction starts out simply and then becomes increasingly complex. As the process builds, and the hits emerge, people's interactions are fundamentally transformed. Buyers and sellers and other players reach a level of interconnectedness in which they undergo a dramatic transition, which some call a "phase change." In biology, this occurs when molecules spontaneously combine to create larger molecules of increasing complexity and catalytic capability. Evolutionary biologist Stuart Kauffman posits that this process of "autocatalysis"—rather than Darwinism—lies behind the mystery of how life evolved. Each level of interaction has its own laws of physics by which the properties behave.

Eventually hits, which appear as explosions, succumb to some form of control. The first application of quantum physics was to create an atomic bomb, whose mushroom cloud lurks for all adults as an image of dark power. Scientists and businesspeople eventually learned to control these explosions to control our energy needs. Another form of controlled explosion involves internal combustion engines, which rapidly oxidize vapors laced with volatile carbon molecules. When these explosions are conducted in a particular sequence they create the rich tonal throbbing of an idling Harley that devotees cherish, a sound so distinctive that it has created a brand and culture.

Or consider the cultural equivalent of an atom bomb: the impact of Elvis Presley. Elvis transformed the nation by radically changing our teenagers' sense of self and the way they formed a community. Suddenly rock and roll became the force around which youngsters dressed, thought, and formed friendships. The fifties were a time when culture was combusted through relatively uncontrolled fads and faddisms. Postnuclear America's culture congealed around such fads as hula hoops, tail fins, and goldfish swallowing.

To paint a picture of how hits behave, we can make a sweeping analogy—replacing people's behavior with atomic behavior, in which individual particles initially bounce off one another in a seemingly random manner until they take on enough energy to "jump" to a new valence with different prop-erties. Learning about what gets the explosion started, how that explosion is kept alive, and how many explosions you can expect in certain environments can help any manager in any industry.

Human Thermodynamics

Markets, hits, and explosions build from the ground up in a non-linear manner—with great and unexpected changes between levels.

These nonlinearities result when *systems* self-organize. The system consists not just of individual pieces, but of the interactions among those pieces and the data that is transferred by those transactions. From such transactions people develop a mutual set of rules together.

Individual parts may operate in a linear fashion, but as patterns emerge, the system as a whole will eventually develop a hierarchy of behaviors. Regardless of whether you are look-ing at a traffic system or a group of buyers in a market, the rules develop not out of the individual behaviors added up, but from the *dynamics of the interacting objects themselves*.

Individual cars on the highway operate fairly rationally. Each stops and starts safely, indicating when they plan to turn or change lanes. Yet when locked in a jam, the group of cars develop a new set of rules. Likewise, individual buyers at Filene's Basement may appear to act rationally when walking calmly through the aisles. But throw hundreds of dressless fiancées together in one container during the wedding gown sale, and a new model of behavior emerges: frenzied shoppers will hoard gowns and swap them with other shoppers while simultaneously waiting to pounce on the discarded options of another shopper nearby.

Or picture a group of young adults who want to go to a movie together. As individuals, moviegoers don't care about the optimal throughput of a system that governs movie attendance. We're simply thinking about the ads we've seen, reviews we've read, or what our friends have recommended. Yet most of the time we attend movies as couples or a group, with an entirely new set of "rules" that are formed for the purpose of attending the movie. Computer scientist Bernardo Huberman, a Xerox research fellow who has studied the dynamics of social decisions, has found that there are two important considerations that individuals in groups face when deciding what movie to see. First, how long will their group remain together? This may affect the willingness of the individuals to compromise. If, for example, the group will see many movies together, then each individual may be more willing to compromise because he knows he will have another chance.

Second, Huberman borrows a construct from thermodynamics called a *stability function* to help explain how each individual's beliefs and wishes contribute to the group's decision. Say it is the opening weekend of *Scream 3*. If one person always wants to see horror films and the others are squeamish, but the horror fan is particularly vocal, then the group may be swayed to see *Scream 3*. The size of the group may also matter—the group may be too large to agree to see a horror movie, and the horror fan may reserve her turn for the next outing. The group may shift into a state of relative equilibrium, with each person initially agreeing to see a particular film. Even if a new person suggests an alternative, like an adult comedy, the group may still remain committed to the original choice.

However, suppose that a second person shows some interest in the new alternative, citing a good review: That might be enough of a trigger to cause the group to recoalesce around seeing the second film. The entire group may respond to this fluctuation and uncertainty and form yet another opinion about whether to see this second film.

And so the individuals in groups feint and parry, mutually forming an evolving and dynamic set of common rules through both cooperation and argument. At any one point, one person's decision can change the opinion of the entire group simply by tilting the direction of the emerging "rules."

This type of collective action isn't limited to movie decision making. Huberman notes that the events that started with mass movements in Leipzig and East Berlin in November 1989 eventually led to new Soviet policies that dissolved the Soviet state. Individual people are reluctant to make their beliefs public, but when a sufficiently large number of people dare to voice their unpopular opinion, a small breakout can occur, which may encourage ever-increasing numbers of people to air *their* dangerous belief. In Leipzig, citizens could go out and protest and risk arrest. But as more people joined, the risk of arrest declined, and the potential to change the government increased as the strength of the protest grew. The most conservative individuals would join in the protest only if there was a commitment by thousands of others.

Similarly, when fads such as 'N Sync, the Backstreet Boys, Britney Spears, capri pants, and Hush Puppies arise, teenagers generally join when it is clear that the object of their interest is also of intense interest to others. People become cool not only for liking the right music, but for being the person who "makes" the fad happen. They have enough influence to create an avalanche of interest that fuels its own spread, cascading through the diverse strata, and in the process chiseling out a common bond.

High School Rules

Consider a highly stratified and highly networked social hierarchy like high school. The social strata are built up as a self-organizing, self-selecting set of decisions of individual students. The weight that one person places on the opinions of others may vary greatly between hierarchical levels. The more active, "hip" strata may have more say in what bands are cool than those in the lower level, who might be shy to express their opinions for fear of being "wrong," or embarrassed, in front of their peers. The level of security that each individual must feel in the strength of conviction he or she has in his or her opinions may vary, and some may be willing to volunteer their opinions only if they feel highly safe from negative consequences. Others may take more risks, balancing the potential reward of increased popularity against the risk of being wrong.

Certain circumstances prompt risk takers to reach out and try to spread the word about the attributes of certain rock and roll groups. It probably depends on how often they listen to the radio, what songs they hear, what stations they listen to, and how often they hear a particular song. These risk takers are most likely not acting as a cohesive unit, yet they are being influenced by common acts such as what disk jockeys on popular music stations are playing. These risk takers may not be a cohesive customer segment, but they each have a set of common tastes and behavior. The risk avoiders might also share characteristics that could be sensed through market research techniques. Although there may be many more risk avoiders than takers, the takers will be far more influential in creating popular groups, which is why recorded music companies are enormously interested in influencing the likes and dislikes of this small but influential market.

These consumers may move toward and away from certain styles of music, like Seattle grunge; the latest perfume brand, like Victoria's Secret's Dream Angels; and dress, like Nine West platform shoes. Those risk takers who determine what is cool in one segment often become overall arbiters of hipness, so that the movement toward shoe style, perfume, and music might converge. Today there are "cool hunters," highly paid professionals who strive to identify tectonic shifts in these platelike demographic strata, in order to get potential hot sellers into the right hands and in front of the right eyes early.

Changes in taste course like waves through these different groups of consumers—at first as small but intense bursts of demand from highly influential adopters, and then from one social stratum to another. Thus hits begin as an individual perception, are transmitted through conversation, and build into the shared beliefs of groups who expect to remain together for a significant period of time. Highly combustible groups, or settings, set a hit into motion and sustain it into a phenomenon that then builds on itself, and grows further from burning its own fuel. That fuel becomes further word-of-mouth stimuli that act like advertising accelerators. Putting a receptive audience in the mood to receive a hit movie, book, or toy is part of the battle; to win the war, you must enhance that excitement with word-of-mouth events.

The power of the media, and its cult of personality, serve as the most effective launch pad for hit products. Ever since little Elliot left a trail of Reese's Pieces (to M&M's dismay!) to lure E.T. back home, companies have skirmished with one another to place their products in highly visible movies. Ever since Tom Cruise donned a pair of Ray-Bans in *Risky Business*, the company has been coasting on that cool wave, one that was reinforced last summer by the shades of Clint Eastwood and Tommy Lee Jones in *Space Cowboys*.

The most dramatic reinforcement of a hit occurs when a notable television or media personality disperses a message widely. In late 1996, Rosie O'Donnell used Tickle Me Elmo in a variety of adventure skits on her popular television show. Immediately, hundreds of thousands of Americans discussed this with their neighbors, reinforcing public awareness of the toy and generating a huge demand for it among kids and parents. Within a very short time a Tickle Me Elmo cult exploded. Tyco Inc. sold over a million units between Thanksgiving and Christmas, and later estimated that it could have sold at least five times that number, given the unfulfilled demand.

Let's assume that each of us has a circle of friends that connects us. Among our hierarchy of friends in this circle, we value several friends' opinions much higher than others. They tip us off to new products that they find intriguing because it reinforces their personal sense of satisfaction. One can imagine hearing numerous stories from people who found Rosie's interaction with Elmo amusing. It's likely that the stories were circulating at such an intense pace that several of them hit any given individual's ear all at once, converting his sense of curiosity into an impulse to actually buy the doll. As posited in John Guare's play *Six Degrees of Separation*, we are all connected to one another.

As the popularity of Elmo cascaded from group to group, the input of advertising and word of mouth contributed to the popularity of the doll in a nonlinear way. Perhaps each advertising impression is not that dissimilar to the individual quanta of light that alter a photosensitive mixture of chemicals: When that mixture receives enough energy, then the energy level reaches a point where each sensitive molecule becomes more likely to transition to another state.

Let's say that there is a fixed point at which an individual buyer becomes stimulated enough to buy the doll. Below that level, there is no buying; above it he is convinced. Whether or not a buyer becomes compelled to purchase depends on whether the overall mix of direct and indirect messages coalesces in his mind.

As we will see more in the next chapter, smart companies know how to catalyze an explosion out of this mélange of direct and indirect messages. Contrary to what many think, companies can't create an explosion by simply throwing huge amounts of money behind every single product. With a large portfolio of films to promote, for instance, studios have to learn to place their bets. Executives who believe they can create or control an explosion are going to waste their marketing dollars. Instead the trick is to somehow catalyze an explosive environment so that the dynamics create their own critical mass. The success of the independent film *The Full Monty* was not due to the amount of marketing dollars backing it. Instead, the studio created enough buzz around the film through exclusive showings at film festivals, word of mouth, and the evangelistic zeal of several key entertainers for the movie to break out into the public's imagination. The Disney Corporation began using the concept "The Full Monday" to promote its Monday night slate. Comedian Drew Carey told the audience on *The Tonight Show with Jay Leno* that he had watched the film three times and loved it. People and forces outside the traditional marketing system were keeping the momentum going, enabling the explosion to be sustained by forces outside the company. When you can identify the system and can work the social network, then you've got the right element to get it going.

E Pluribus Novum: How One Plus One Equals Not a Number

As individual agents aggregate into groups, and groups come to form dynamic markets, the combined interactions of consumers or other agents change in an unpredictable manner. This shift in behavior is characterized by nonlinearity; you cannot divine it by simply adding up the dynamics of the group and assuming the new mixture will simply reflect this formula. Like magnetizing particles that become collectively aligned during magnetic induction, people who may be independently stimulated by marketing actions undergo a permanent shift in how they are connected to one another.

Some scholars have attempted to give a name to this condition. Hermann Simon, a consultant and visiting professor at the London Business School, describes "hysteresis" as a phenomenon in which a combination of temporary conditions such as regulatory changes or price cuts may permanently affect a company's market share. Of course, market share should be seen as a total property—like a traffic jam—that describes the aggregate changes in purchasing behavior of individuals.

When Philip Morris lowered the price per pack of Marlboros several years ago, for example, it immediately gained a spike in its market share—even after competitors retaliated by cutting prices. After a pharmaceutical company set its prices above the government-established reimbursement amount, it lost ten market-share points. Three weeks later, management cut the price to the reimbursement level. The company never regained market share, despite the lowered price.

Overstating his case only slightly, Simon says, "Virtually the whole of social behavior cannot be satisfactorily explained without hysteresis." This phenomenon helps explain the underlying mechanism by which groups of consumers who cluster around a hit build to new levels, and are collectively changed.

Groups of consumers in markets that are sparked by a hit product's energy will act like charged particles that are "lifted" to a new energy barrier. In the old state, both individual consumers and the collective system have been resistant to change. Yet pump in enough marketing dollars sufficiently quickly, and the group receives a "shock" that permanently alters the market-share fortunes.

Simon argues that several factors must come into play for this effect to happen. "First, a favorable external situation must emerge, which a company must *spot early and interpret correctly* [my emphasis]. . . . Then the company must take an unusual, innovative action to surprise its competitors and prevent or delay their reaction. . . . The action should possibly be accompanied by heavy signaling, which could include bluffing to prevent quick competitive reactions." Simon correctly points to examples in which companies shock the market by, say, introducing western cigarettes in Germany, but more is at work. The most powerful shock to the system is the effect of word of mouth. The social fabric that drives consumer decisions underlies the dynamic portrayed in his model. This emergent word-of-mouth phenomenon begs for a closer look.

Individual Actions Performed at a Distance

The basic building block for looking at the emergence of a hit is the notion that the things we buy are ego-driven artifacts. Products don't become hot sellers because people buy in isolation; they heat up when we as buyers begin to meld "who we are" with "what we buy."

At the most basic level, we embody the very things that become our hits. As consumers, we reexperience our lives and build our identities through the ego-driven artifacts that we buy, own, and consume. Certain hits, for example, reward us by providing nuggets of memory and aggregate to form who we think we are. I might like, say, Steve Miller's 1969 anthem "Space Cowboy" simply because the tone and melody sound good to me. Or it could be that the song takes part of me away from my current surroundings and reminds me of who I thought I was when I was in high school years ago. In that case I'm attached to the memory of myself that the song triggers more than the melody itself, and I replay those feelings of how I remember I was whenever I listen to the melody of the song.

Physical artifacts also carry this hidden, though nearly palpable emotional, association. Do I throw away the pen my friend gave me in college because it is balky? Other pens in my writing jar may be far more useful, yet I keep this pen as a sentimental reminder of who I once was.

This identification with an external product plays deeply into one's decision-making process in, say, buying a car. Most of us like to believe that we cull the best information on big decisions from consumer magazines in an effort to pick rationally, when in fact this decision is wildly prone to inner considerations. Say I am a Chevy man. I've bought Chevys in the past, and even have a Chevy insignia on a belt buckle. Yet the new look of the F-150 Ford or the V-10 Dodge Ram may turn my head. Or as Tom Hanks says in *Nothing in Common*, "I look good in a Jeep." We are RAM tough, Trail Blazers, Bronco men.

What we are saying is that our self-image is built of the brands and products with which we identify. But it is not only the image we project to others—it is something deeper. It is the image we project to ourselves. This deeper image is ultimately the sense of style we have: who we want to be is how we build the construction of who we are. If we reflect on Oscar Wilde, who said that the most important thing is style and later said that the most unimportant thing is style, then we have the paradox in essence. What we have is an obsession with style, or, in Southern California terms, we want to be cool and really *be cool.*

In such a manner I tend also to recognize the patterns of a product's packaging and, if the brand is familiar enough, will fill my garage or shopping cart with what I assume will continue to provide a high level of satisfaction. The resiliency of brands depends on the ability of consumer-goods companies to cultivate this type of personal identification with a product. For example, I buy Tide detergent and can always recognize its distinctive packaging of bright yellow, orange, and red. No other detergent looks quite like Tide. The box calls out from others at a glance, even from a distance. I choose Tide almost reflexively, and have since freshman year in college. That's when I made the choice to buy the product, and I have now internalized that decision as part of who I am. I no longer have to think about this action.

For the vast majority of products that I purchase, I am an excellent pattern recognizer. I have formed an expectation of what those packages will provide. As long as those promises and expectations are not broken, I will continue to remain a loyal buyer. Over time, in fact, it's likely that I will forget exactly what converted me into a loyal brand consumer. Rather, I will continue to buy the same brands because I have programmed myself to do so. This is no longer a conscious or logical decision, but one in which my by-now-unconscious decision completes a pattern of my behavior that has persisted for some time.

A driving force in my unconscious decision to buy familiar products is a chemical system in the brain called *dopamine pathways* that connect package patterns to an expected reward in product efficacy. The dopamine system in our brains is a neurotransmitter-mediated set of pathways that appears to transmit all of our memories and action-response triggers. But even more important, dopamine helps us learn. When stimuli from the outside world are measured against our expectations, our brains dole out a bunch of dopamine, which evaluates whether or not the stimuli exceeds our expectations. Thus we are not merely responding to the outside world, but to that rush we feel when a previously confusing concept clicks into focus. This "Aha!" can be experienced as the recognition of a familiar product that fulfills my expectation, or the satisfaction received when experiencing a new insight. That's the rush from a little squirt of dopamine.

This pattern of behavior can also be changed. Each of us stimulates our own system every time we meet a goal we've set for ourselves. Changing individual consumers' behavior can permanently alter their expected dopamine reward. And this calls for our unconscious learning mechanism to be sufficiently stimulated so that it permanently reaches a new conditional learning state.

Remember our quanta of light? If I am a reactive liquid in a vessel, and I get stimulated by new light particles and absorb their energy, I might change my properties. Maybe over time, if I'm left in the dark, I will revert to my previous state. But I might change permanently, and really have no hope of reverting. I might be involved in a one-way conversion process.

And what if these small but additive particles I absorb were not light particles but commercial advertisements? One commercial probably wouldn't register. But if I see five in the span of two days, I might become stimulated to the point where the message of that commercial becomes consciously or unconsciously embedded in my thinking. I may be compelled to take some action. If I continue to see thirty more impressions in the next five days, I might grow tired of the commercial, and close myself off to its message.

The real magic starts, though, if I am additionally stimulated by sources other than the commercial itself. Say I have a discussion about the commercial with my friends or family and am encouraged to purchase a product. While I may believe that I am acting on my own accord, on the basis of what I like, I am actually factoring in how others will perceive my purchase—and me as a result. In such a manner, the tacit yet negotiated approval and opinion of others becomes a consideration in what we buy.

Take that new Swatch, for instance. Do I add it to my collection because it is distinctive from the others I have and reflective of the fashion statement I want to portray? Do I buy a coat because of the quality of cloth and the warmth it gives me on cold nights—or because of how I think it makes me look to others? Do I buy at Barneys, where the salesperson may know I like striped shirts and Jerry Garcia ties, and where she makes it her business to make my experience simpler and more satisfying, or do I buy elsewhere?

Once home, I find my choice subject to another whole framework, with a different set of conditions, or rules. I might ask my spouse if a certain tie goes with my suit, or if it fits in with my collection. I have begun to trust my spouse's opinion over time, not to just tell me what I want to hear, but because I think that she knows what I like and don't like. I have come to expect that input as part of my own decision-making process.

Over time people either build up a level of trust in others' opinions or begin to dismiss them. They might just assume that they'll never see that person again, and they are selfishly motivated or programmed to behave in a certain way. Over time, I've built up a trust network with individuals: friends who see movies early, and whose opinions I've found, over time, to be a good predictor of how I will feel about the same film. College roommates have an innate ability to pick out great books long before anyone has heard of them.

This notion of trust is bound into the way we communicate through things. I wear symbols of artifacts in this world I've become attached to. I may have bought the Disneyland sweatshirt because I was cold, but I wear it again and again to show others that I went there. What we buy increasingly becomes a message of who we are to the people we trust. And so as consumers building trust and making friends through these networks, we base many of our purchasing decisions not on what we know we like, but on what we believe others want us to consume. This excerpt from a news article written several years ago provides an example of how groups make such decisions:

> Little Tree, a coming-of-age story set in 1935 Tennessee, was rousingly received at a screening for college students. But in a discussion that followed, audience members conceded they probably wouldn't see the film.
>
> [Producer Jake] Eberts said he told them, "I'm intrigued that you embrace this film when you'd buy a ticket to Con Air before you'd buy a ticket to this."

They said, "We know all our friends would see *Con Air*, and I have to tell my pals I've seen it, too." (*USA Today*, November 24, 1997)

As additional dynamics are added, deciding which products to buy becomes ever more complex. Individuals build in more and more criteria—conditions and relationships that deal with myriad personal and external qualities—when considering why they buy certain items. This is where game theory becomes relevant. Game theory is often used to describe the possible actions that individuals, companies, and other groups in a particular situation might take. Game theory looks at how the outcomes of interactions between players are affected by the structures, or rules, of their market or environment, and the beliefs players have about each other's behaviors. These rules are mutually constructed, emerge from the behavior of the individuals, and are therefore relevant to complexity. We will explore this dynamic in greater detail in chapter 5.

Power Laws and Fractal Landscapes

There is one more law that provides a frame for these individual stories, one that helps to address the question of how hits happen again and again, over time and over many different markets and environments. This law also helps managers address such questions as the following:

As fads begin to flicker and die out, how can businesses fan the flames and keep the fire going? How does the flame fade away? What am I going to do to my business so I can recognize, affect, and profit from these explosions?

Earlier I mentioned how small quanta of light can permanently alter mixtures of billions of molecules in a cascading reaction; so too can one memorable commercial or television appearance simultaneously change the minds of many people—even if we aren't in the same room, town, audience, or frat party. The light particles, or advertisements, that change a group's mind appear to be random. Yet because each advertisement seems on the surface like the one before or after it, the reason that that particular advertisement broke through the clutter and caused a permanent effect seems to be that it came at the right time. We would of course assume then that the resulting number of hits, and their size, would appear to happen randomly as well, leading to a hopelessly and totally unpredictable process. Guess what? There may be predictability in the randomness itself.

Although hits may be caused by a random process, the number of hits that occur within a particular context may not be completely unpredictable. Power laws are the fractal curves found in most natural events like earthquakes. In a period of time, in any seismic area, there will be many tiny earthquakes, a few moderate-size ones, and if you are (un)lucky, a huge one. The Richter scale is built on this power curve, as is the scale associated with storms in weather forecasting. In each of these natural phenomena, there are many little events, and fewer big ones. The curves that describe the number of events over time are self-similar at different scales; no matter where you look in terms of time or in magnitude of the event, the curve remains the same.

Cultural quakes also seem to happen in a fractal distribution. That is, huge explosions seem to be followed by smaller, more controlled pops. No entertainer is likely to ever have such an effect as Elvis because he was a catalyst of an explosive nature; all other performers follow in his wake. Today, for instance, we live in a post–Tickle Me Elmo world. Fresh on the heels of Tickle Me Elmo, Children's Television Workshop licensed a "Sing-and-Snore Ernie" to Tyco Inc. for 1997—a product that was more complex than Tickle Me Elmo (remember how products and systems become more complex?) and which, despite enjoying an even higher rate of sales during the holiday season than Tickle Me Elmo, received much less public attention. As we shall see in chapter 5, seasoned managers leverage this power law to insure that, over time, their portfolio of products enjoys sustained profitability.

It is fascinating to note that we can use the rules of quantum physics to explore the phenomena of Elvis and Elmo. But this is because hits begin as simple transactions and over time become complex, adapting into new systems. In that regard they can be analyzed with the theoretical tools of complexity. Some of these tools draw from thermodynamics, and help us understand the dynamics of huge quantities of related but independent entities, like atoms, molecules, and groups of people. Like atoms that are shaped by an outside magnetizing force, people are attracted by and coalesce around such forces as advertising. Fully charged and energized, like atoms receiving full quanta of energy, we are compelled to purchase. And we do. As detached, free-thinking actors, we as consumers appear to be the masters of our own buying behaviors—yet we are influenced along with millions of other consumers by not-so-random triggers that sometimes encourage us to become hit makers.

Moreover, like tunes that stick indelibly in our minds, the echoes of past explosions linger in our culture to affect how we experience and relate to current events. Recently the composer of the short musical introduction to *I Love Lucy* passed away. For years, he didn't want his name associated with that new phenomenon of television. And yet his singular creation triggers a response and an expectation in millions of people who will always associate it with what became classic comedic acts. He was playing his part in forming an emotionally grooved pathway that influenced—and was in turn reinfluenced by—all subsequent comedic television.

Humans aren't atoms, of course. And maybe we shouldn't think of ourselves in that way. But these techniques do help to explain the most unpredictable phenomena we encounter in business, that which seems so mystical and elusive. At the atomic level it makes no sense to gauge our cognition and recollection about Lucille Ball, or Tickle Me Elmo, or Hootie & the Blowfish. But aggregating atoms into humans helps us to understand our individual reactions and our group behavior if we see it "at a distance." Some companies have learned how to harness this atomic energy, not for nuclear fission, but for human fusion. Let's look at how you, as a manager, can start to try to harness this energy as well.

3

COMPLEXITY AS COMPETITIVE ADVANTAGE

Let's go surfin' now
Everybody's learnin' how
Come on a safari with me

—THE BEACH BOYS

Surfing represents a massive fantasy for many—and a nifty metaphor for managing in a complex adaptive system. That's because all the associated activities of surfing, from preparing to do it to reveling in the dreamy post-surfing state of getting psyched to do it again, serve to inform managers how best to survive—and thrive—in the choppy waters of their industry.

How does one surf? First, you prepare by building a mental model of what's ahead. You talk about the hottest beach's activities with friends, or chat on the Web with others who share your passion. You might dream about the waves the night before. And then when the day comes, you physically prepare by driving to the beach, waxing your board, donning your gear, and paddling out in the water.

Then, drawing from your skills and experience, you see when the right wave approaches from the sea, and suddenly— boom!—you are riding it. Balancing and veering, staying with green water, outside the foam, calls for great tactical knowledge, which enables you to stay with the wave as it changes shape and direction.

And when the ride finally ends, you wait and watch, preparing to go again.

Nonlinear Jumping

As we saw in the previous chapter, hits build from the ground up, and are shaped by the way that people form groups around ideas and products. Like a group of cells that suddenly comprise a conscious system, these groups then cluster together and take on characteristics that are profoundly different from the sum of the parts. Moreover, the group's actions are *nonlinear.* They seem to occur as surprises, defy logic, and result in a fundamentally different mix of behavioral components.

What, then, is the job of the manager? To get the waves pumping at your beach? To learn how to ride the waves that you see on the horizon? Or both? It seems paradoxical, and in fact contradictory to the bottom-up, self-organizing state of complexity to suggest that one can actually *manage* this adaptive process. To do so would imply that it is possible to impose top-down orders that could hammer the system into compliance. In fact, the essence of managing in a complex system is recognizing that complexity *can't* be managed. And so the manager's role is not to reduce complexity over time, but to some-how make sense of this simmering stew.

Understanding how hits emerge from complex adaptive systems by identifying patterns as they emerge in real time provides managers with "levers" to pull or push—tools that can tilt the dynamics of a system or inject enough energy in the right place to start an explosion. Managers and leaders who learn to guide explosions of demand with marketing "shocks" can dislodge competitive incumbents and gain lasting market share. And companies that are subject to increasing-returns economics—those in emerging markets, for example, or high-tech industries—can "tilt" the dynamics of an industry so as to insure that their success builds upon itself.

This chapter will look at a number of specific tactics and strategies that will help managers better understand the present, forecast the future, turn emerging forces to their favor, and in the process produce hits. In particular, managers can learn to visualize patterns as they emerge, and in so doing, recognize when a system is subject to change.

This perspective will enable you as a manager to take high-leverage actions that yield disproportionate results. Because nonlinear outcomes are determined by small, chance events, managers who realize when change is about to occur can realize significant leverage. Like the judo master who uses his opponent's weight against him, or a surfer making small positional adjustments to stay afloat on a wave, managers who know when and how to apply this kind of pressure will realize huge payoffs.

These specific forms of leverage include catalyzing an

environment so it is ready to combust, applying a "shock" to the system that starts a chain reaction, and, on a broader scale, using game theory to one's advantage—that is, developing a contextual understanding of the interactions, mutual dependencies, and shifting dynamics of an industry can maximize a company's future.

Smart managers are like great surfers who have mastered the process of identifying and riding the right wave. Much of the work involves preparation: Just as surfers get ready by dreaming about their activity, talking with others, learning what the weather is like, and developing an intuitive ability to find the best wave, so too do managers begin to gather the right data, recognize patterns, see where systems are ready to break, and build in the ability to create a wide range of futures. And there are many tactical skills shared by both: Surfers develop an innate knowledge of how to shift their balance, how to veer and coast. And managers who learn how to anticipate how and when the foam is breaking surf the waves of demand in their markets most successfully.

From the Simple to the Complex

As an industry evolves, its products, processes, managerial belief systems, and consumer habits evolve from a simple to a complex state.

To illustrate this idea, economist Brian Arthur likes to compare potato chips and computer chips. Potato chips started out simple and remain simple to this day. Potato chips contain potatoes. Computer chips, on the other hand, started out relatively simple and have evolved into something quite different. Since their first introduction, the number of transistors in the chip has increased exponentially, as has the corresponding functionality. A chip now includes subsystems, cache memories, numerical processors, DSPs, and the like. Software is another example. Microsoft Word, which began as a relatively simple program to use, has become positively baroque with its endless options and features.

Even less high-tech products, such as cars, go through this "complexification." Henry Ford prided himself that the simplicity of the Model T enabled its owners to practice their own repairs. Likewise, one of the great selling points for the Volkswagen Beetle was its simplicity. The fact that most people could open up the hood and fix the car appealed to millions of consumers and, in fact, led to the bestseller status of VW repair guides. Today cars are a completely different story. With their computerized dashboards and automatic transmissions, even a sophisticated driver often needs the help of an expert to diagnose the simplest of problems.

Once upon a time in the telecom industry there were very simple rules for pricing. But over time, the rules of interaction among buyers and sellers of telephone service have become dauntingly complex. When the Bell System held a monopoly fifty years ago, phone customers had no choice. A residential customer who wanted telephone service had the "choice" of buying local service from Ma Bell, who would rent them a black rotary phone and bill them monthly.

Today those rules feel quaint and anachronistic. When a

residential customer requests phone service today, the phone company offers countless competitive services ranging from call waiting to voice mail to caller ID, all with a plethora of pricing options and supermarkets of available phones for sale—or lease. And if, of course, the customer wants a second line, then the company repeats the variegated options, and then some. If the customer wants Internet service, for example, this introduces a whole new range of options.

Today no mathematician could write a formula that neatly describes the dynamics of this transaction. Years ago the formula was a simple if/then proposition: *If* the customer wanted service, *then* the phone company provided a simple product at a simple price. With the level of complexity that has crept in, only a colossally complicated equation could account for all the different options and contingencies of this transaction. Over time a huge number of events ranging from the Carterfone regulatory decision to the popularity of the Princess phone to the entrance of MCI and Sprint into the telecom wars has caused the environment to grow and evolve into a fundamentally different system than it once was.

Not only are products subject to increasing complexity, but so are the manufacturing and marketing processes as well. Coca-Cola, which was once sold in familiar eight-ounce glass bottles, is now available to the customer in a variety of packages, from the ubiquitous can to the two-liter plastic bottle. In addition, there is the explosion of related soft-drink products, Diet Coke chief among them—all of them naturally in both caffeinated and noncaffeinated varieties—not to mention Coca-Cola merchandise from bottle openers to sweatshirts. In support of these brand extensions, the company's promotional savvy and ubiquitousness is extraordinary, tied to everything from the Super Bowl to national movie theater chains.

Developing a Schema as a Response to Complexity

People respond to ever-growing complexity by developing an internal and often implicit set of rules about how to cope—a set of rules that gets increasingly more complicated as the business does. In his book *The Quark and the Jaguar,* physicist Murray Gell-Mann calls this belief system, or way of understanding the world, a "schema." Gell-Mann argues that every human being operates as a complex adaptive system with an evolving schema about how to behave in the world. "Whether putting together a business plan for a new venture, refining a recipe, or learning a language, you are behaving as a complex adaptive system," he writes.

These schemata might appear simple. Somebody seeking a taxi in New York will learn to flag down only those cabs with a light on. As he adapts his schema over time, he will develop an understanding of where to find cabs with lights on during peak hours, and how best to catch their attention. Eventually, as other would-be fares cluster around this prime hailing spot, the first seeker may adapt her schema to find a spot that is more fruitful. An example of a more complex schema would be the collective actions of individual traders and entire groups conducting trades in the stock market.

Managers create schemata through which they navigate their competitive environment. As managers deal with business they generate rules about how best to operate—in their individual department, corporation as a whole, and industry at large. These rules help them make sense of the world. Like the buzz we get from our dopamine pathways, creating a schema feels good because it somehow helps us to explain the world we live in and convinces us that the unpredictable is predictable.

But as the system in which managers operate becomes more complex, these schemata must be constantly renewed and adapted. The following principles suggest a few ways that managers can do this. As a system tends toward more complexity, introducing elements that appear as random, the job of the manager is not to distill the complex into simple terms. Rather, it is to refine one's schema to embrace the advantage complexity offers.

Visualize and Recognize

The first technique useful in dealing with complexity is learning to become a good pattern recognizer. This entails gathering and responding to data *in real time*. All too often managers are burned by the lag time between the data they collect and its useful half-life. By the time they compile and make sense of the information, it is no longer relevant. Many companies miss great opportunities due to the lag time between "information collection" and action.

At PricewaterhouseCoopers, we have worked with USWest, for example, helping them to understand better the implications of their daily transaction data to determine the extent to which they can meet and counter changes in the competitive landscape with marketing and sales force action. Heretofore this information has been short-circuiting the information systems. People might have had a hunch that something was happening, or they might have heard it from other salespeople. But the "system" reported information only at the end of the month when the transaction data was rolled up and classified. With information systems that engage at a more granular level and reflect local, technical information to the people with the power to act immediately, they could respond faster and better.

Don't Hide Your Hits

As we learned in the first chapter, more is different.

Yet the tendency of many managers dealing with data is to produce a single number from a true series of discrete events. A sales manager, for example, will look to annual trends to plot strategy rather than finding the more meaningful demand that takes place over the course of a month, or even a week. The key to spotting nonlinearities is to disaggregate—to recognize and isolate the spikes or drops in demand, and see what they indicate.

For example, the administrator trying to maximize service at a hospital may average out the traffic flow of patients over the course of a month. This may suggest that the average cost of inpatient care is rather high. But a closer look at the numbers would show that on virtually every Saturday night there are several gunshot wounds and perhaps another catastrophic accident—pushing up the costs dramatically. Averaging out the costs over the month will hide the "hit" that indicates the Saturday-night bubble of demand.

Early noise may not be static, but a real signal of coming change. Tim Fohl, a research executive from Sylvania and GTE, has found through studying the dynamics of innovation that progress occurs in an S shape—early progress erupts into a huge innovation that then tapers off. As Thomas Petzinger writes in *The Wall Street Journal,*

> Though a new technology advanced in small steps in the beginning, it did so with big swings in performance between individual successes and failures. The greater the variations early on, the steeper the slope of the progress that followed. In other words, it appeared that major errors and false starts at the beginning forecast a higher score in the end. Tolerating—even encouraging—a wider range of possibilities early seemed to nudge a project toward a steeper takeoff.

Managers thus need to pay closer attention to their details. By taking a good hard look at the data and recognizing the "pops," you can find indications that a real opportunity is presenting itself. In recorded music, for example, one song that appears to be a nonevent on the national charts may in fact be enjoying a great run at a handful of radio stations. This could indicate great demand demographically or geographically, and can tip a marketer off to change strategy, reallocate advertising, or commit more marketing dollars to build the hit into a regional sensation that may indeed eventually find its legs.

Recognize When the System Is Ready to Change

Physicist Per Bak has come up with a word to describe the near-chaotic state achieved when a combustive mix of elements is poised to change into something new and altogether different: "criticality." A pile of sand on a table helps illustrate this phenomenon. As each new grain of sand is added to the pile it grows and grows, causing some sand to run off—until at one point one new grain of sand causes a major runoff. This notion of a seemingly stable system that is actually poised for collapse characterizes criticality, where one simple change can foment fundamental transformation.

In his book *Would-Be Worlds*, journalist John Casti posits that even the Roman Empire reached a state of criticality:

> Of special interest for us is the path by which the Roman Empire collapsed. Basically, this path involved an ever-increasing level of political and economic unity, coupled with external challenges bringing the Empire to the critical point at which the cohesion of the Empire actually begins to decrease while the challenges continued to grow. Prior to this point, the Empire was able to rise successfully to the various external challenges from invaders and local warlords and maintain a high level of central domination. But at the critical point,

the system was poised at the knife-edge of collapse, and it took only a very slight outside challenge for it to be overthrown, thereby rapidly sending the Empire into a state of subjugation.

Business systems also approach criticality. One sign of this may be a temporary capacity overload that a company can't immediately absorb. Though this is more likely to occur in businesses and industries where the use of information technology has provided companies the ability to extend their traditional ways of doing business faster and faster (in turn accelerating their ability to fail spectacularly should they be unable to recover quickly from an inability to meet demand), even traditional businesses run up to the point of criticality.

Take railroad evolution, which in the United States is going through a rapid consolidation. Much has been written about the recent woes of Union Pacific Railroad, which could not easily assimilate the 1996 merger with Southern Pacific that turned it into the nation's largest railway. The merger of the two railroads pushed the entire system well beyond the capability to handle its load. With too few locomotives, freight cars, and engineers to handle the increased demand, the company simply stranded cargo along major stretches of its rail system. Companies that had become reliant upon the efficient transport of goods through Union Pacific's network encountered delays that equaled damages of up to $1.3 billion.

When the expected length of passage was measured and expected to be weeks, the overall system had enough slack to absorb the peaks and valleys of demand. But as these peaks became more numerous in time, the system had to evolve in order to handle the new amount—and rate—of demand. The peaks came in a fractal mode. That is, there were many small peaks of demand on the network, few large ones, and very few huge ones. This same distribution was hugely accelerated by the merger. When railroad networks were combined, the collective peaks and their frequency were even larger and ever more numerous. The system to handle this distribution was forced to the limits of its capabilities.

The Union Pacific system extended beyond the locomotives, engineers, and cargo. Ships backed up at the edge of Los Angeles Harbor because the entire railroad system was choked with cargo, and overflowed in grain elevators in Texas. When Union Pacific became too complex to manage, these extensions of the network also failed catastrophically. This type of collapse could begin from failures in other companies with similar network externalities—any of the telecom players such as Bell Atlantic or MCI-Worldcom.

Certainly, not all managers need concern themselves with such huge systems. But they do need to hone their antennae so as to be prepared to identify criticality as it presents itself in their own business.

Take High-Leverage Actions

Spotting trigger points such as when a single is about to hit the charts, or when a rail line is running to capacity, or when a small but passionate fan base for a certain item of clothing (say

Hush Puppies shoes) is about to coalesce into a fad, can enable managers to achieve a fundamental principle of complexity: leverage.

Because complex systems are often poised at the edge between chaos and order, and hits pop out when the elements of a system reach critical mass, managers can realize disproportionate gains by discovering where a market or system is prone to leverage. Small inputs can be amplified throughout a system to have a major effect. One familiar example is a vaccine. "A small amount of an incapacitated antigen, say the measles virus, can stimulate the immune system to produce enough antibodies to make us completely immune to the disease," points out scientist John Holland in his book *Hidden Order*. "The vaccine 'levers' the immune system into learning about the disease, saving the costly, uncomfortable procedure of learning about the disease 'online.' "

Likewise, smart managers find ways to stimulate a system into naturally spreading its products. Energizing evangelists represents one form of leverage. Finding and marketing to the most reactive demographic groups is another. And creating a hit that changes the competitive landscape to one's particular advantage represents another.

This involves developing a fine-tuned understanding of how specific shocks, like marketing, will affect consumers. Some seasoned managers have developed an acute sense of this, deducing over time whether their competition will try to dissipate the energy before it is absorbed by customers by sending out dampening waves to reduce the shock.

Different consumer groups naturally have different levels

of tolerance to this shock, or what scientists call conductivity. Some are more willing to accept the shock and respond to it, and some will reject it. Some shocks may travel over previous pathways of lowered resistance and therefore enjoy little friction. Others may run up against a system that has already been shocked and is not oriented to receive much new energy. Teenagers, for example, are a particularly reactive group.

Managers must also track how patterns form across different consumer groups. When does a breaking hit spill over from one influential group to a less active group? Finding this trigger point can help determine when to crank up a marketing budget, or find a new way to tap into an emerging network of consumers. For rap music, for example, the music scored an explosion of success when it crossed over from predominantly black audiences to suburban whites.

In Japan, for example, fads appear to burn up and burn out much quicker than they do in the United States. This seems to be more a product of demographic distance than geographic distance. That is, the fact that the population is clustered together quite densely and is therefore in greater proximity with one another seems less relevant than the fact that Japan's relatively homogeneous social strata are more permeable than in the United States, where links are less aligned and interrelated.

Last summer, we conducted a research project with Hakuhodo, a leading advertising company in Japan. We studied one of the fastest-moving consumer markets in the world: J-POP music, Japanese music aimed at teenagers and young professionals. In this market, the entire product life cycle can play out completely in one month. We wanted to compare the effectiveness and accuracy of synthetic consumer models that we had developed in the United States with models of Japanese consumers.

The enormous popularity of J-POP music is staggering, and the speed of new act development, promotion, and hit creation—and dissolution—is mind numbing. If inventory is needed anywhere in the country, CDs can be manufactured, packed, and shipped overnight. We still don't have the MP3/Napster Internet-mediated generation of free music services we expect. But today in Japan there is a healthy rental market for CDs, much like videotapes, DVDs, and game cartridges in the United States. The reason for the rental market is simple. Karaoke is so prominent that teens rent a CD single, practice for hours at home, and emerge a few days later to mimic their favorite stars in private Karaoke rooms with their friends. The draw of Karaoke is just one element of the hyperspeed dynamics of this pop teen market, but it clearly helps get hits started.

Added to Karaoke is the way individual CD singles appear, and then are aggregated into albums, which then have more of a guarantee of acceptability among fans. Also, fans are barraged with a panoply of promotional vehicles: sidewalk and in-store contests, blinking electronic displays in trendy, hip stores, Tower Records chief among them. And publications are religiously read and studied. People hunger for the latest news and hover, giggle, and explore the insights of the new title and artist. And when hits happen, these amplifying forces can combine to form colossal followings:

GLAY consists of four mop-top musicians (sound familiar?) playing to a very involved, frantic four million of its closest fans in the single largest concert in the world to date.

The challenge we had was calling hits from duds early enough so that savvy music execs who, in some cases, had seen the evolution of the Japanese music industry since before the Beatles could benefit. In the end, our prototype program did admirably. We created 50,000 Japanese teenagers (synthetically, of course) according to their buying habits, artist preferences, and musical tastes. We studied the market using two months of control data, where we could track the known sales of a wide range of artists. Our model predicted the sales of new artists and titles for a month, and called hits from also-rans in over 75 percent of the cases. In addition, by examining radio airplay, retailer expectations, mall research on teens, and reaction to promotions, we were able to predict the timing and magnitude of the hits usually within 20 percent of the actual sales totals. We were encouraged to examine other consumer markets in Japan to determine whether we could use the same simulation methods to predict sales of toys, video games, television shows, cars, and even construction equipment. Indeed, we have discussed converting these market models into a "virtual Japan" resource for market research, product introduction, and new product development.

Japan's fast-moving markets may give a glimpse into a highly evolved consumer system of purchasing behavior; compared with our models of U.S. markets, we found that teens are more responsive to a wide range of promotional and marketing stimulants, compared to the nearly total reliance on radio airplay in the United States. This may give a glimpse into the future evolution of some of the most successful e-retailing behaviors, where websites integrate knowledge bases with traditional brick-and-mortar sales channels and "humanized" shopping experiences into their offerings. The look into Japan may be a peek into the evolution of purchasing behavior as sales move at the rate of "Internet speed."

Create Communities and Enlist Evangelists

Hits spring from fast-forming networks that are sparked by "hot" products or ideas. Therefore the key for a manager is to identify where word might spread fastest, and help build or create these networks. Smart managers exploit the natural or synthetic connections among people who use their products, asking the question: What is the visible or invisible tissue that connects consumers to the product, and to each other?

Avon Products, for example, enlists business associates to help sell products. Movie studios and record labels count on the fan clubs that spring up around hot TV shows or stars to propel the popularity of a hit. Even the commonality of technology users around a product such as Windows 2000 forms a network: every successive buyer of Microsoft's operating system ensures the probability that more people will support this standard.

One of the best examples of a company that has consciously developed an adaptive network is MCI's "Friends and Family" marketing program, where the company gave its customers an incentive to build their own networks of loyal users.

Introduced in June 1991, this innovative campaign tapped into an idea with a long tradition: Find an incentive for customers to find and create more customers on their own. MCI offered customers who converted twenty other "friends and family" to MCI 20 percent off their phone bill when speaking with those in their circle.

This seemingly simple concept rested on the ability of the company to manage a highly complex database of customers—to be able to track which members belonged to which network, and whether they would realize their discount upon calling. More important, many experts attributed the success of the campaign to MCI's ability to infuse this new relationship with nostalgia—to find the emotional spark that personalized long-distance service for customers, turning the campaign into a warm, even hip word-of-mouth phenomenon that enabled the company to increase its market share by two points in the first year of the campaign, enjoying $1.2 billion in additional revenues.

Companies that find and exploit these generative networks can gain a disproportionately positive advantage from their efforts. These networks can become pathways, in essence, through which marketing messages can thrive and gain exponential exposure.

One of the more powerful ways to exploit a network such as this is to enlist "evangelists" who will further energize the most reactive demographic strata, fanning embers into a flame. These product users might "pop" with the slightest provocation and provide fuel to the word-of-mouth explosion among first movers.

High-tech companies such as Apple Computer or Palm

nurture their evangelical base by enlisting the help of rabid users. They send their most devoted fans Beta versions of software, knowing that these users will not only provide useful feedback to the company, but will likely spread positive word to their own networks. Other companies, such as Nike, enlist the help of professional "cool hunters" to track down the hard-to-find early adopters—the coolest of the cool kids whose simple act of purchasing a new athletic shoe may spur increasing cascades of demand among fashion-conscious buyers.

Surfing the Waves of Demand

Preparing for waves of demand and then capitalizing on them are two forms of action managers can take to help create hits. There are other actions that address the competitive landscape—moves that help one compete in the broader context of a complex market by literally changing the rules and dynamics. Having a grasp of these principles can help managers find and ride the waves of demand in the marketplace, and sometimes shift the dynamics of an industry to their advantage.

Perhaps one of the most important tactical lessons is the importance of placing an early stake in the ground in an emerging market and then leveraging that position. Companies don't always have to be the very first to market to control the market. But they do need to be a quick study of what is happening in that market and have the ability to adapt their processes and products to fit.

Companies in increasing-returns industries such as software can place a quick, "dirty" stake in the ground early as a means of helping form the grooved pathways to their advantage. Innovators thus let the market help them adapt the product and make it malleable. Perfecting it in the lab first is the best way to kill the product, whereas starting a conversation about the product, and enabling users to adopt and then adapt the product, begins to build the grooved pathways that insure success. In the early days of software development, this sometimes meant announcing a product even before it was commercially available.

First movers don't always win, but it's important to be early, to adapt quickly to these rapid changes, and to grab as much territory as you can, whatever this territory might be. Many companies have capitalized on being the first to market: Intel, which leads the chip industry by obsoleting its own products through relentless innovation; FedEx, which literally invented the express package industry; and CNN, which continues to remain the leader in twenty-four-hour televised news. Yet the list of failed first movers is also impressive. Fuji, for example, invented the recyclable camera and yet has lost the lead to Kodak, which has done an admirable job of branding this product by producing everything from underwater disposables to kids' throwaways. And of course Microsoft, which didn't invent the MS-DOS operating system that launched its dominance, serves as the best example in today's economy of the fact that you don't always need to be first in to own the market. Those companies that prevail are the ones that gain sufficient mind and market share so that success builds upon itself.

The best strategists understand the art of surfing. Good surfers don't just catch the first wave; over time they have built up radar that also tells them which wave will give them the longest ride. Moreover, they know how to move from wave to wave in the nimblest and most effective manner. Surfing is all about tipping points: tiny movements and shifts in weight that tap into how the wave is breaking.

One of the most important techniques a manager can use is to *inject complexity into the system that you alone can manage best.* Injecting manageable complexity into a system can help a company shake up a market where one product reigns. Marketing innovators simultaneously dislodge habitual patterns of stimulus response from the minds of consumers while replacing them with a new stimulus-response pattern—in which consumers purchase their product instead of their competitors'.

When telecommunication giant MCI started in the late 1970s, it didn't have a complex, evolved system. Unlike AT&T, which had built into its technology thousands of service order codes, MCI was able to build computer systems that were unburdened by a deep legacy. As such, MCI could introduce the revolutionary Friends and Family marketing campaign. Because it could manage the complex system better than AT&T, it could produce simpler bills for consumers. AT&T simply could not effectively, directly counter except by discounting everyone.

AT&T had painted itself into a corner—building up a high level of complexity driven by the historical model of universal service. MCI, on the other hand, started simply, without all the baggage. MCI allowed customers preferential treatment and in so doing started fresh and simply without the baggage of the past.

At the same time, companies must avoid the dark side of complexity. Keeping systems and processes and products too simple invites competitors to knock them off—and yet there is a real danger of making things so complex that everything blows up. As evidenced by Union Pacific Railroad, complexity can build and build until the system hits a critical point of catastrophic failure with no chance of rapid recovery.

From Strategic Planning to Strategic Positioning

Finally, given how fast change happens in a complex system, smart managers rely less on long-range planning than on betting on a series of short-range tactical moves and finding the ways to create grooved pathways of success. Why spend money and resources on a five-year plan when it makes more sense to *make* the future you want? How, then, can you change the rules of the game, the boundary conditions, that enable you and your company to emerge as the winner in a dynamic field?

Consider how America Online pulled itself out of the once-crowded Internet-service-provider industry to become the undisputed leader today, with more than twenty million subscribers. The company managed this feat through a series of brilliant competitive tactics. A mere decade ago, there was a handful of players in the field. Yet AOL rose above its rivals to become the clear winner of the online-services war by managing complexity better than the other players.

When the company first began to take off, in the early nineties, it did so by attaching a very human face to the Internet. It developed a complex software that made the online experience simple and friendly. Unlike competitors such as

CompuServe or Prodigy, AOL was easy to use. Many of the early zealots flocked to the service because of the burgeoning use of "chat rooms"—networks of passionate early adopters who in turn formed an expanding web of market externalities. Later, as the Net became a more viable consumer option, AOL responded by offering a flat rate for service and providing its expertise as the best to make sense of this new world. Even the company's technical growth was informed by an understanding of managing complexity. The business system was not a massive top-down system but one that grew to accommodate the growing market of customers.

Understand the Context for the One Right Action

Again, this calls for a systems approach—trying to understand not merely who the competitors are and what they are doing, but how the entire industry is developing, both competitively and cooperatively.

The notion of coevolution helps explain why certain hits explode at certain times. Consider the fax machine, a technology that lay dormant for more than a hundred years until becoming ubiquitous about fifteen years ago. Why did the fax machine, after so many years of being around, suddenly rise in popularity in the early eighties? Because of the coevolution of Federal Express, which gave consumers another option and opened their worlds to see the benefits of fast delivery.

Sun Microsystems' successful development and launch of

its computer language Java represents a great case of a company incorporating many of these principles to their competitive advantage. How did Java, as CEO Scott McNealy put it, become "a bigger brand name than Sun"?

Several years ago, Sun developers took a floundering programming language code-named Oak (initially designed for interactive TV and handheld devices) and presented it to McNealy, who saw in it huge potential—something that could fundamentally change the computer industry.

McNealy and his colleagues revamped the computer language to address far broader applications. Unlike other computer languages, Java was designed especially to run on a network, by using applets (small programs designed for specific jobs). Applets can be stored on the Internet (or any network), so that the end user downloads only what she needs, eliminating the costly, time-wasting effort of loading software and its upgrades onto the desktop. This helps developers animate networked programs with the sort of moving, interactive graphics that are usually available now only on CD-ROMs. This language was an easy-to-learn, just-in-time software that provided an opportunity to convert differences between old software programs, including decades-old legacy systems. This language also gave many large companies an alternative to products such as Microsoft's Windows NT software that were designed for more powerful servers.

Sensing a wave that the company could ride to success, McNealy and his team implemented some key and very shrewd decisions. They named the language Java, a hip term that seemed to endow it with a personality. They positioned it for desktop PCs. And they used the then-nascent but steamrolling Internet as a platform for their success. Sun released the product for free on the Internet, and in January 1995 the company cut a deal to package it with the dominant Web browser, Netscape Navigator. Kim Polese, Sun's director of marketing (and the current CEO of Marimba Inc.), conceived her role as broadcasting excitement along with the product.

Sun quickly built on the spreading success of Java by reinforcing its foothold. The company soon began sponsoring Java-specific conferences. It created a subsidiary called Java-Soft, to listen to and cater to the needs of the onslaught of Java programmers. JavaSoft created Java Workshop, a tool for helping make writing Java programs easier for programmers. In 1997 Sun announced it had set up two hundred Java design centers to provide technical consulting services to software developers and information technology engineers.

Today there are more than 400,000 Java programmers. And the success of Java is in little doubt. A survey of 279 corporations found that, in the next few years, 97 percent will use Java for server-based applications; 84 percent will develop new applications in Java; 75 percent will use Java to extend the life and usefulness of existing applications; and 21 percent of corporate spending on software development will be Java-related. Java may be the first time a software language has crossed over into pop-culture fame: Nescafé even asked Java inventor James Gosling to be a spokesman for its instant coffee.

Sun profited handsomely from Java—not simply from licensing the Java language, but by selling the servers and software to companies hopping the Internet wave that Java helped propel. A recent survey found that roughly 35 percent of all the WWW servers in the world were made by Sun.

Java benefited from three coevolutionary facts: (1) the rise of the Internet craze. Web developers were ecstatic over the idea of applets, which could operate over computer networks and were relatively safe from viruses and other security risks. (2) Corporate computer executives were realizing cost savings through networked computing. (3) Computing firms were looking for a way to chip away at Microsoft's monopoly. As Lotus president Jeff Papows was quoted in the November 11, 1996, *Fortune* magazine: "I am the second-biggest Java fan in the industry, behind only Scott McNealy. Why? Java will be instrumental in loosening Gates's stranglehold on the world." Indeed, Java may have made the Sherman Anti-trust lawsuit against Microsoft irrelevant.

According to McNealy, most of the "high-concept" strategies that he has used are borrowed from other industries. "Our whole concept of the computer as a network device is grounded in a business model that was stolen from every other large utility on the planet," he says. "You don't have a power-generating plant in your home; you're connected to a power grid."

McNealy developed a business model that reinforced Java's position. According to chief technical officer Eric Schmidt, now the CEO of Novell, "We showed Scott [McNealy] the technology and described how we might want to work with partners to give it broader appeal. He saw it as much more, as a destination for the whole company, and even for the whole industry to pursue. It was like a switch went on."

Before long Sun had developed a keiretsu-like network of supporters, including IBM, Oracle, and dozens of smaller outfits. Kleiner Perkins, one of Silicon Valley's premier venture capital firms, hastily pulled together a $100 million fund to invest solely in Java start-ups. Polese, the former director of marketing, formed Marimba to help Java become even more powerful. Like Java, the name Marimba has connotations of vibrancy.

Java was developed in a house in Vail by a group of Sun engineers that wanted to develop a computer language that would allow software developers to produce programs that could be written once and used on any computing platform. That this group would attempt to develop such a language is surprising enough, but that it would succeed is even more incredible. The language owes much of its syntax and grammar to the popular programming languages that preceded Java, including C++, C, and Pascal. But putting it into the hands of developers who would embrace it, and later into the heart of commercial code that could be sold as end-use applications, was the real trick.

The Java team used the principles of increasing returns to guide the launch and development of the nascent market for Java into a hit. The Java team had sensed a large wave of demand on the horizon with the growth of the Internet, and the networking of large quantities of servers on the World Wide Web. They had lived with the coevolutionary power of object-oriented code and fast processors that could allow one type of computer to effectively emulate another. And when this team began to sell Java, they did so at a price that was easy to afford, with advantages that were tough to match for free.

Sun managers had successfully found and ridden the waves of demand for Java. Today, of course, there is one powerful tool that further enables managers to discern and act upon waves of demand, and in so doing create hits. That tool is computer simulation. By tapping into synthetic customers for insight, managers can take even more effective actions in producing products that rise above the choppy waters of the market to become the familiar hits of our lives.

4

NATURAL ADVICE FROM THE SYNTHETIC WORLD

[Artificial life's] promise is that by exploring other possible biologies in a new medium—computers and perhaps robots—artificial life researchers can achieve what space scientists have achieved by sending probes to other planets: a new understanding of our own world through a cosmic perspective on what happened on other worlds. "Only when we are able to view life-as-it-could-be will we really understand the nature of the beast," [Chris] Langton declared.

—M. MITCHELL WALDROP
Complexity

It's late one evening in the small town of Treewell, Vermont. Most residents have finished work, done their daily shopping and their daily chores, and are nestled snugly in their beds on this cool autumn night.

One Treewell resident, however, burns the midnight oil. He's the owner of the local private loan and real estate business and he's going through his personal finances. His purse is full, to be sure—the normally quiet town has recently seen an upswing in the business cycle. A few new shops have opened in the last several months, and he has reaped the benefit of the real estate transactions that necessarily preceded the new stores. He smiles wryly—these new shops are now undercutting each other's prices in order to secure the loyalties of new customers, which will lead to a few bankruptcies, and then more real estate transactions. That's the—what did his granddaughter call it, from that movie she's watched a hundred?—oh, yes, the Circle of Life. Or certainly, he thinks, the Circle of Treewell.

Still, a surly frown gnaws at the recesses of his wizened face—the money that he makes does not completely satisfy him. He's a longtime resident of Treewell, member of the town council, and a devoted land preservationist and environmental activist. Most of his personal gains have been spent purchasing land throughout the town—not for development, mind you, but in order to preserve its natural beauty and the scenic vistas that are ubiquitous throughout Vermont. He owns the largest amount of land in the town and fiercely defends his right to do so. He's even bought land surrounding the covered bridge that proudly guards and majestically heralds the southern approach to Main Street, even though selling the land to the owner of a gas station would fatten his purse considerably.

This evening, however, he's faced with a dilemma. An offer lies on his desk, expressing interest in acquiring a small parcel of land on the edge of downtown, a parcel that he owns. He's not sure what the potential buyer wants to do with it, but he suspects a new outlet store for one of those fancy New York clothing boutiques. If he sells his land, he suspects that Treewell will *see more tourism, which is always good for business, but also suspects that more people will want to move to Treewell as well, which means more growth and overutilization of the already fragile land. Yet the amount of the offer is attractive—with that money, he reasons, he could purchase five times that amount of land on the outskirts of the town and preserve it forever.*

He makes up his mind to wait until tomorrow to decide whether to sell. After all, he decided to sleep on it the last two times something like this happened. Never mind that he sold both times. This time, he might decide differently.

I'm watching Treewell as I write this, spotting the cyber-residents as they purchase their silicon goods and inflate their electronic prices in their computer world. That's right, Treewell represents a highly advanced version of an artificial world that we at PricewaterhouseCoopers created in order to study emergent behavior.

How do you learn about complexity in our natural world? By building an agent-populated artificial one. The very nature of the dynamics of complex adaptive systems calls for new tools of understanding. As John Casti, professor of operations research at the Technical University of Vienna, writes in his book *Would-Be Worlds*:

> Each of the processes sketched above is an example of a complex system, one consisting of a large number of individual agents—investors, virus molecules, genes—that can change their behavior on the basis of information they receive about what the other

agents in the system are doing. Moreover, the interaction of these agents then produces patterns of
behavior for the overall system that cannot be
understood or even predicted on the basis of knowledge about the individuals alone. Rather, these
emergent patterns are a joint property of the agents
and their interactions—both with each other and
with their ambient environment. The ability of such
systems to resist analysis by the traditional reduc-
tionist tools of science has given rise to what is
called the sciences of complexity, involving the search
for new theoretical frameworks and methodological
tools for understanding these complex systems.

These new tools are the artificial "would-be" worlds of computer simulations.

By setting synthetic customers into motion with one
another, one can glean insights into a complex system that are
far more surprising and robust than one can gain from observing our "carbon-based" world. There are many reasons why. By
providing time flexibility, artificial worlds enable us to recognize patterns in myriad business metabolisms—enabling one to
back time up, slow it down, and turn it around. By comprising
virtually every possible outcome among the complex interactions of players, artificial worlds help us ask better "what-if"
questions. And by enabling us to observe equations as they
emerge from the ground up, artificial worlds help us recognize
patterns in real time—affording people what John Holland
calls "lever points" that realize disproportionate effects.

Although conventional business tools such as spreadsheets or regression analysis can provide tremendous value to managers, they are and will always be *linear approximations of nonlinear events*. Though they provide tremendous analytic value, these tools fail us when we most need them—at the moment when nonlinear changes occur, when it feels like the ocean suddenly ends and a cliff appears. Years ago, I consulted with Nevada Bell, which like all telecom companies is faced with fierce competition from all sides. My job was to persuade senior executives of one potential outcome: that the company's market share definitely could drop below 60 percent. This fall from near-monopoly status was inconceivable, simply beyond their imaginations. Yet computer models helped show that yes, this future could still happen.

Models allow us to broaden our viewpoint beyond our fixed notions, based on current reality, of what can transpire. These scenarios help expand our linear expectations to include all the possible futures we may encounter—which, as I will explain later, directly contradicts the traditional model of consulting.

Moreover, computer simulations help people who are all too often (and with good reason) afraid to tamper with real systems, since even the most preliminary tests may create unforeseen or unintended consequences. Models, on the other hand, reveal potential outcomes—without any harmful consequences. And in fact, the robust simulations now possible enable us to produce models with substance and relevance.

For example, software developer Ken Karakotsios, who

helped create the Simlife game, has designed a chemistry-set program for high school students to learn how to make chemicals like mustard gas and chlorine. The Bunsen burners can be digitally lit, are tied to a digital gas stream and put under an icon of a beaker that has a mixture of benign components that can produce the noxious gases—without harming the student. This may sound straightforward, but has true value for all of us who have had to evacuate organic chem thanks to careless colleagues. Likewise, one can't underestimate the importance of trying out business changes in a practice arena before these changes are put into the real world.

Today's computer simulations exponentially expand our capabilities to foresee possible outcomes. In his book *Emergence*, John Holland describes how the breathtaking evolution of computing power has enabled people to create and inhabit an infinite number of potential scenarios. As a young scientist in the fifties, Holland and his colleagues first explored models with the available technology: paper and pen. Yet as the first rudimentary computers opened up the potential of modeling, Holland and his peers found themselves speeding up the process enormously. Today computers are of such speed and power that they can quickly reveal the behavior in a complex system and create thousands of potential outcomes that derive from the same starting point, with the same set of rules.

Understanding the Market from the Ground Up

Computer simulations built as complex adaptive systems offer a fundamentally new approach to understanding how a system behaves: from the ground up. With their ability to replicate the step-by-step and often unpredictable process by which agents like humans interact, simulations help shed insight into emergent behavior and its attendant nonlinear events.

Many people have tried to represent how a market works, for example, by writing equations that represent stocks and flows. Yet the actual workings of a market are generated through a more intricate and less predictable set of interactions between consumers and advertising, buyers and salespeople, or consumers and the overall sales environments. It is impossible to understand how the market behaves by looking at it from the top down. As properties aggregate, they change. Over the years, for example, economists have produced countless numerical analyses on the generation of queues. They all provide a straightforward set of equation-driven models. While many provide an equation that describes how groups of people cluster into lines, none analyze how these individuals learn and adapt as they form queues.

In previous chapters we have seen how emergent behavior is often decentralized, adaptive, and emanates from both the agents in a system *and* their interactions. This type of emergence simply cannot be understood or represented by taking a large system apart and then putting it back together again. As Chris Langton has asked somewhat facetiously in his lectures, what do you get if you dissect a squirrel and then put it back together again? Certainly not a live squirrel—but a mess. Therefore in our work we don't seek an equation that describes the market: *We try to enable the market to describe the equation.*

Systems Thinking

This type of approach butts up against classical systems thinking, a school of thought developed by engineers who sought to understand how, in a large system, various energies and actions could be causally linked. Based on Newtonian physics, this school seeks rational solutions to phenomena, and is appropriate in closed systems of simple behavior.

From the point of view of the scientist or mathematician, however, complex or nonlinear systems are a logistical nightmare because most cannot be understood analytically. Often no set of equations can be posed and solved to relate the characteristics of a complete system. Even when one can gain some understanding of how nonlinear systems work, they often remain unpredictable. However much one understands stock markets or the properties of sand, it will still be impossible (in principle) to predict the timing of a crash or a landslide. The only generally effective way of exploring nonlinear behavior is to simulate it by building a model and then running the simulation.

A closed system is surrounded by a tight membrane or boundary, where all the forces that define the actions of that system are contained. Innovation may have a lot or a little to do with the existing competitive rivalry. Does innovation arise spontaneously, over time, like the in-bottle fermentation of a fine wine? Not usually. Innovation arises from the interaction of rivals that are contained within a bottle; while it takes the combined efforts of the agents, innovation reflects more than simply their aggregated qualities.

In trying to make economic sense of the world, economists have relied upon the attributes of closed systems to help define interactions and constituents completely, and to attach a deterministic outcome (if this happens, then that will occur) to interactions within the system. This closed system is familiar to economists who describe the world in a mathematical model of a series of equations. A closed system can settle down toward a steady state of equilibrium—where things happen in a relatively linear fashion. Even Michael Porter's model of strategy draws boundaries around the internal rivalry among competitors, with external forces (say from suppliers or buyers) upsetting the balance.

The fundamental myth behind many business analyses is the notion of the equilibrium position, or steady-state. Analysis is meant to determine conditions, and especially causation in the equilibrium state. Yet far too many models—most prominent among them Michael Porter's competitive diamond—assume that business conditions are independent of time. Emergence shows that the environment is time-dependent. Probably the most dangerous and fallacious of all the hidden assumptions in business models is that today will be the same as tomorrow and every day thereafter.

To find the boundaries of hidden assumptions, we can alter various aspects of a model, such as the rate of time, to find hidden patterns in company and industry behavior, like times of peak activity. By changing the resolution or fidelity or time-step, one can take large things apart and see the structure underneath. There is now a movement afoot to formalize this synthetic approach to performing science that differs markedly from the "scientific method" we've all come to depend upon.

For a telecom company like SBC, it means understanding

fundamental competitor behaviors, and examining unusual trajectories of "future history" with the onset of full-fledged competition. It means creating an explicit knowledge about the set
of assumptions and entry strategies and financial assumptions
from the competitor's point of view. And it means preparing for
guerrilla warfare, understanding the importance of the unfold-
ing of competitive dynamics as events occur, and not predefin-
ing the "battle plan" for one all-out "assault."

Where are we going to find this evolutionary process of
selection if we, as builders of these worlds (in our heads or in
computers), don't define them with equations? We need to turn
the job of strategic selection over to the world itself—to build
a world with the coevolution of problems and solutions. Strategies are not good or bad in and of themselves—what matters is
who we're playing our strategic games with, what they know
and don't know, what they think of themselves that may be
true or myth, how good they think their strategy is, and how
likely they are to change it.

Overall, these artificial worlds, and maybe the real worlds
they are trying to emulate, set their own boundary conditions—they self-organize, maintain homeostasis, and build
structures that can adapt, like companies. Maybe Chris Langton is correct when he surmises that we may be evolving toward
an ecological mixing of humans and machines in organizations.

In our work, we have sought to build models of these artificial worlds that explore these problems. We have tried to
avoid using equations that define systems thinking as proposed
by Professor Jay Forrester and his followers from MIT. We set
out to let the equations write themselves, and for the dynamics

of the market itself to determine the outcome. What we did not want was some external boundary condition developed by a human programmer to taint the experiment.

The alternative, digital world would probably feel more familiar than the world inhabited by rational thinkers and optimizers who live in equilibrium. These worlds would distinguish individual actions from macro-based impersonal markets. Agents that have different styles of thinking and different histories of experience, and act in a social structure where independence is coupled with social convention and cultural rules, would inhabit the artificial world.

In their book *Growing Artificial Societies*, social scientists Joshua Epstein and Robert Axtell argue that the advent of such powerful computers, coupled with our understanding of emergent behavior, points the way for a new, generative social science:

> The broad aim of this research is to begin the development of a more unified social science, one that embeds evolutionary processes in a computational environment that simulates demographics, the transmission of culture, conflict, economics, disease, the emergence of groups, and agent coadaptation with an environment, all from the bottom up. Artificial society-type models may change the way we think about explanation in the social sciences.
>
> What constitutes an explanation of an observed social phenomena? Perhaps one day people will interpret the question, "Can you explain it?" as asking, "Can you *grow* it?"

Indeed, such a question is now relevant to an understanding of hits in the business world. Here's how I came to learn of this process, and what has developed since.

Ground Truth

Years ago, I was a geologist who interpreted satellite images of rocks and vegetation, a field called remote sensing. Part of the challenge in this field was accurately interpreting images taken hundreds of miles from the objects themselves, which were much smaller than the field of view. The resolution was poor, and individual objects like houses, cars, driveways, and people were mashed together in a blurry continuum that had to then be pulled apart and classified as suburban neighborhood, golf course, mall, and the like. In a way, it's not too different from the classifications and interpretations we as humans make of the world around us. At a glance, I can identify a '57 Chevy from a '56 or '58. I can tell an authentic Googie-style coffee shop like Norm's on La Cienega in L.A. at fifty miles an hour. I can also link these two objects into a period landscape representative of an era long ago. When the resolution begins to blur, classification becomes difficult—categorization becomes harder and harder. What makes the Chevy and coffee-shop signatures recognizable is the ability to take a selective ground truth sample—to occasionally dip down and know for sure what is there, to examine a small example in order to make a wider, more sweeping interpretation.

In our attempt to build a lifelike population of virtual customers, we view primary research as a mechanism of remote sensing that is accompanied by confirmation of ground truth. This quality can be built in through the use of incredibly specific and robust data. Our approach differs from traditional research techniques. We have developed a powerful computer simulation program that is designed to capture and make sense of ground truth. Our program contains a population databank of over 250,000 synthetic individuals—silicon-based "people" who represent real people and their purchasing preferences in a variety of extremely detailed categories. Cognitive scientist Andy Carr of Washington University in St. Louis calls people "fast pattern completers." We are really wonderful as humans at completing patterns. We get a hint and then fill in the rest. We see a black tail swishing around a corner and we assume it is a cat. We get a whiff of water upwind and we assume there is a spring nearby. Our very survival depends on this way of thinking.

We have endowed our artificial humans with the same fast pattern-completion capability. These artificial agents don't know everything, but they can smell something in the wind. Of course, they don't have the full cognition of human beings. They can't multiply two numbers. But that's not cognition. In addition to these capabilities, these agents have primitive emotion states, and they have small but important demographic differences. In aggregate, these differences add up to the enormous variety of reactions to product introductions—in other words, to the buzz that can produce a hit or a flop.

The profile of each silicon-based individual starts as a real person who answered questions about what type of clothes, dishwashers, or beer they preferred, why they bought certain items, and when. We thus create a set of purchasing patterns tied to demographics. So, before we add any cognitive capabilities to these individuals, we capture an accurate pattern of behavior that is both statistically valid and is demographically representative of a sample population of the United States. We build an artificial world that contains these digital buying signatures, each one imbued with the characteristics that reflect what real people said to interviewers at a point in time about particular buying habits. We stuff each response into the memory of individual digital consumers. Each agent then represents the exact beliefs and attitudes from the time when that interview was conducted. We don't mash the individual answers into categories, market segments, and cross-tabs. We keep the resolution at the ground level. This enables us to combine the respondent's demography with the primary research response. We can match beliefs, attitudes, and demography on an individual basis, and create a population, a society of individuals who reflect what real people said they had done and were going to do, and why.

Starting with this vast artificial society, we then use a digital version of the claw from the movie *Toy Story* to pluck out samples from this population. Often we gather a group of buyers from a particular locale—say from Albany, New York—to see how what they had bought differs from another sample— say Abilene, Texas. Each of these interviewees is part of the ground truth. We know what interviewees said they had done and would do. We then can clone these individuals, change their gender or age, mate them with one another to create families, groups, and couples. We can then create disembodied memory banks that we can attach to cognitive engines that can drive future decisions and create emergent markets.

In one case, we sampled the ground truth about consumer buying habits and listening history of a number of retail stores and radio stations across the country. We wanted to reexamine whether we could create an accurate historical pattern before we endeavored to project the future based on our population-growing technique. We used this primary survey information to form the kernels from which we grew a population of synthetic individuals that embodied these buying and listening habits. We then compared these samples with remotely sensed actions from the real world through scanner tapes and airplay records. In comparing the remotely sensed actions of our artificial buyers with the remote sensing signature that classified the actual buying public in the real world, we were able to ask whether real humans did in the artificial world what they said they would do in the real world. We were also able to determine whether the artificial world was indeed a reflection of the real world, and in either case, we were able to find out why, down to the individual level.

In the real world, we have only the tools of remote sensing and ground truth available to us to sense phenomena as they occur. Look in the wrong place, at the wrong time, with the incorrect resolution, and you can miss the formative stages of patterns. With our actual senses of sight and hearing, we can sense broad vistas and listen to remote calls, and with our ground truth senses of taste and touch, we can sample tidbits and remnants of data. We can broadly gauge market-share changes and sample the shift with mall research and exit polls. Yet we can make sense of these different sensorial methods only through the inference that ties ground truth to remotely sensed images of the whole.

So too in the artificial world, we can remotely sense the emergent phenomena of markets as they arise and decline. We can perform ground truth tests against individual synthetic buyers that cause markets to take off or fall flat. In this sense, we can study models of causation of emergent phenomena that are rarely possible in the real world, where longitudinal studies of consumer behavior may be impractical. In artificial worlds, the notions of remote sensing and ground truth are extended to the visualization of emergent phenomena that arise from coordinated actions of groups of artificial individuals. And, because these buyers reside in a computer, we can conduct experiments on them, take advantage of our ability to alter our resolution and focus, and so more directly manipulate time and space.

Metabolism

Business metabolism is not simply about "moving faster." Rather, it's the ability to alter the time dimension to suit the phenomena we are dealing with. Altering time lets us reexamine the past slowly or quickly and rapidly play out a tape of future events that might take years to unfold in actual wall-clock time. The rapid uptake of sales in a simulated recorded music fad may either whiz by unnoticed in a flash or become too static. But at the right pace the hit appears as an exploding burst of buying, full of structure, rich in detail, and worthy of comment.

With the use of simulation technologies, our companies can metabolize, or digest, rapidly updated states of the world without becoming too full. Companies or managers that become overwhelmed with data will often set it aside, complaining that "there's just too much." Now they can begin to get their arms around this data as a whole by starting with bite-size snapshots of the world and breaking them down into more easily understandable nuggets.

The snapshots are not averaged over months, but retained as reference points, important dates—the days that mattered right before and right after introduction of a popular lipstick color, for example, including the sales taken in during the hours that the introduction of that hot color first began. Each snapshot would record possible departure points where causation could have played a factor. We can look for what causal factors could have been in play at that time. Maybe it was the color on the cover of *Vogue* that week that got people interested in that shade. We can also ask, "What if the departure point took us here instead of there?" For example, what if Buddy Holly and James Dean had lived into middle age? Would we have seen a British Invasion? Would James Bond have appeared as a defining cultural icon of the sixties?

Time travel or time flexibility is a big notion that is wrapped up in metabolism. Also included in this idea is the spatial or geographic resolution of observations—the relative amount of detail (often geographic) covered in a particular observation. Think of a department store that is gathering data on employee performance. Building an operational model with one sales total for all stores per month is a fundamentally different notion than several observations of the number of sales per square foot per day or hour. Each different level of resolution leads to a different view of how the company operates: its physics, its cause and effect, and what lever can be pulled effectively to gain or lose strategic advantage. The same set of principles in a geographic sense can alter the notion of cause and effect and the degree of tactical advantage from store-level, department-level, city-level, or national-level analyses.

This time flexibility affords us the opportunity to capture hits and potential hits as they emerge, in even the least likely— or most nonlinear—scenario. In the computational world, simulations allow the ability to conduct many simulation runs, to fine-tune the parameters and find unusual outliers or stories to be remembered. Totaling revenues monthly effectively destroys the patterns that are seen within the month. Looking at the year on a monthly basis removes hundreds of possibly revelatory daily observations, and thousands of hourly observations. Even saving the snapshot of one day recorded every minute might be instructive for understanding how the whole year behaves.

The complexity of a hit recorded-music album, for example, can appear random, say on a DMA (Designated Market Area) scale, where each minute of time in the model equals one minute of real time. On the other hand, the same phenomenon can appear as part of a well-behaved pattern at another scale. Play the tape back faster, with each minute lasting a few microseconds, and see if a pattern emerges. At a perfect pace, a hit can appear as something more familiar.

When the pace of change is rapid, as in a hit situation, the number of purchases accelerates rapidly from a low level and can take place too rapidly to get a handle on. "How do I stop time?" was one of the first questions asked by our TeleSim executive simulation–game players. How about slowing down time, so that the pace is more to a timing we are accustomed to? Or speeding up time, so that a year takes a minute or two?

Consider a traffic jam. As you move up from the level of individual cars along a road to a full-blown traffic jam, you see a pattern emerge. Similarly, one finds that hits have a common pattern, one that emerges from their individual actions. When that same set of interactions among cars is spaced out in time, the pattern is lost and appears random. The essence of the traffic jam emerges at a certain scale. Notice how when time is speeded up or slowed down the patterns become more recognizable. Devastating earthquakes can appear to be random, and on a human time scale, they are. But near Palmdale, California, major earthquakes occur about every two hundred and twenty years. Exactly when the next one will happen is not known, but on a scale of thousands of years, the regularity is easily seen.

The schema we build up to make sense of the world takes these time-scale and resolution differences into account, as we make patterns out of the subtle regularities that we see every day. Hits come and go in a variety of speeds and sizes, and when we can slow down or speed up time to explore these hits and discern their patterns of regularity, we gain a better knowledge of causality and how the world works.

Simulation is necessary to speed up or slow down the metabolism of a company and allow us to see patterns that might otherwise go unnoticed. Metabolism is the rate at which we divide time, coarse or fine. In a simulation, we can speed up history, freeze it, store memorable moments, and recall them when we need to.

Putting Our Agents to Work

In 1993 we developed the TeleSim management training simulation program with software developer Thinking Tools. The simulation essentially melded the Maxis game simulation SimCity with the first rudiments of agent technology. This simulation was designed to help guide the helms of telecommunications company start-ups that wanted to grab market share and profits from incumbent Regional Bell Operating Companies (RBOCs) such as Pacific Telesis and NYNEX.

Our foray into the world of training simulations and computer games whetted both our and our clients' appetites. We received the message from our clients that to be more useful and meaningful, we needed to address real business issues with real data. That required an entirely new and more powerful computer architecture, orders of magnitude more powerful than the Intel 386–based PCs we were using in 1993.

We looked at the world of business and determined that the forecasting of hits in industries such as the music industry would be noteworthy. Cracking the code on how to distinguish hits from run-of-the-mill releases early in their life cycle would be a difficult place to start building detailed models and simulations. We knew that standard numerical techniques such as regressions were terrific at finding the historic trend and providing a forecast of linearly increasing or decreasing sales. But musical CD sales trends were anything but linear, and this was where our new technique could take a run at the more established methods.

We were interested in tackling the seemingly chaotic music business, where success seemed to accrue to those executives with an instinct to find, nurture, and sustain hit songs, artists, and labels. So we sat down to produce a model that would reveal how people buy CDs, and how hits in that industry got started. With the help of Scott Page, then an economist at CalTech, and Rob Bernard, who joined Coopers & Lybrand on Halloween 1995, we put together a prototype model to use multiple agents to show how sales dynamics of a single album changed over time. Specifically, the program was to address the question: How do word of mouth, prior experience with a band, and quality of an album contribute to an album's success?

Each particular album had several variables: what demographic target it was aimed at; what its musical genre was; the critical acclaim it received; and finally, quality (a notoriously difficult variable to measure that we ultimately came to dispense with).

The model contained two hundred consumers. They were heterogeneous; that is, each of them had different characteristics. Each consumer had a specific demographic profile, a preference for a particular genre of music, a level of interest for each band, and a certain number of friends whose opinions they valued. Each consumer used the album's perceived quality and an individual weighting of the four variables (closeness of match of demographic target of album to the consumer's demographic profile; closeness of match to preferred and actual genre; how much the consumer liked the band in the past; and the consumer's trust in the critics) to come up with an initial value that represented how much the agent wanted to buy the album.

Next, we put the simulation into motion. During each time-step of the simulation, the agents talked to one of their friends and exchanged information regarding their thoughts about the album. Then they changed their opinion (or didn't) depending on how much they trusted that particular friend's opinion. If an agent reached a certain threshold value, it purchased the album.

When we ran the simulation, we were amazed at the depth and meaning we could get from such a simple model. In almost every simulation run, there were several agents that bought the new album right away, without talking to their friends or taking any other actions. When we looked at these agents more carefully, we discovered that they had an almost fanatical devotion to the band—these were the real fans that would buy the band's new album no matter what. This was a real phenomenon—one that emerged in our model without our specifically programming it in.

The real problem with this model was the fact that each album was assigned an intrinsic "quality" that influenced the final quantity of sales that the album had. We were determined to try and dispense with this variable and had several ideas for doing so: using reviews in music magazines to indicate quality (the problem here was that not all albums are reviewed, and reviews, of course, are inconsistent); using quality not as a constant, but instead trying to estimate it from the slope of the takeoff of the sales of the album (i.e., using word of mouth to estimate quality); and using pre–album release listener opinion surveys from the music industry (the difficulty here was that this information is highly proprietary and guarded). In the end, we decided to dispense with quality altogether.

Obviously, in the real world these products have an

intrinsic appeal. Content matters. But it is greatly amplified by the social transactions these models portray. And it is these amplifications that make all the difference.

When we ran our first model, we saw agents buying albums, and eagerly looked to see whether hit albums indeed would occur in the program's simplified approximation of the world. In this initial crude implementation, we saw a group of one hundred or so buyers respond to the stimulus of a recording's movement on a synthetic Top 40 chart and to the word of mouth about that rising song that spontaneously generated a hit. The mechanism and results looked plausible, and the mechanisms of word of mouth among these simple adaptive agents seemed to produce an emergent hit. But to demonstrate how these agents could reveal how hits were produced from the bottom up, we needed real recorded-music sales data, fine-grained enough to fill our computational forecasting mill and real enough to be convincing to music executives.

The source of this data was in the electronic files of SoundScan managed by Mike Fine and Mike Shalett. Sound-Scan data are the source of music industry sales trends and the *Billboard* charts of top performers. We wanted to determine whether we could differentiate those CDs that would become hits from those that wouldn't. And we needed to test whether a hit would occur by using real albums that had already turned into hits. We also wanted to show how quickly after release we could tell a potential hit apart from a record that would turn in a so-so performance.

We built a series of small, discrete memory banks into each agent, each of which could store a dozen or so important experiences. These experiences took on the flavor of "I was in this restaurant and heard our song playing, and I remembered the time I first heard it with you." Perhaps an overly romantic memory for a piece of silicon, but in any case there were some agent-resident memories that for whatever reason also were important enough for the agent to remember. Each of these agents had four sensorial mechanisms, to put it into biological terms—they could listen to a radio station, hear other people's conversations, look at a CD's placement on a Top 40 chart, and watch how many records had been sold in their record store. They could update each of these memory banks daily with new memories, and could attach each of these experiences to the particular CD they were referring to, whether from chart placement, airplay, number of retail sales, or conversations.

Our agents are motivated by one thing: to be the first to spot a trend and to "call it right." If they do, they come to the notice of their peers. They wanted the social reward of making the right predictions that they could tell their friends about. Through these successful predictions, these agents attract more and more followers to listen to their prognostications. Each agent was a self-motivated, pattern-seeking predictor of musical trends that wanted to spread the word to obtain a following. And we could vary the level of risk that each agent could take. Agents could choose when they would start telling their friends about a hit that was in the making. It was up to their individual risk-taking profile if they wanted to go out on a limb. If one agent was particularly attuned to a small but notable upturned blip in sales volume, and if this agent was sufficiently motivated, it could tell its friends about the change in sales trend. In short, we had a thousand little selfish predictors making up a single forecasting tool.

And these agents were acting more with their guts than with deep analytical thought. They were little emotional beings, pieces of artificial life with primitive brains that were motivated by their position in the social structure that was of their own making. They lacked a set of rules about what was good music, but wanted to listen to music that was already popular or what they thought would be popular in the near future. And they could get a greater degree of reward if they were among the first agents to label a particular CD a hit before others became aware of the inevitability of it. But their obsession with popularity was a double-edged sword; if the agent was wrong in its predictions, then it might be viewed as a social outcast by its peers and its future predictions might be ignored by the very friends it wanted to remain popular with. Agents wanted to be proven correct when it came time to realizing their predictions; they wanted confirmation by legions of other agents that paid attention to what they said was cool. If the agents could say that a particular CD was cool, and they turned out to be right, then they became a little cooler themselves. If they thought that something was cool, and didn't get up the nerve to talk about it with their friends, they would be less admired, and had no basis to say I-told-you-so.

Besides the innate motivation to become popular, these agents could also learn and remember. The agents used a tried-and-true learning method—a 500-million-year-old algorithm design, derived from the learning system of the honeybee. This system, similar to the dopamine learning system used by humans, was described by Terry Sejnowski of Scripps, who gave a great lecture at the Santa Fe Institute as a part of the learning-in-economics program. Terry had studied the social structure of bees and how they learned; he found a similar type of cognitive learning pathway in humans. He also found that humans and bees approached risk taking in roughly the same way. In modeling human behavior in these forecasting programs, we knew we had to severely abstract human behavior down to the barest essentials. But we found a link between human and bee behavior, primitive as it may be. So we made our agents little bees, seeking flowers in the form of CDs that could give enough sugar to stimulate the learning system to remember that this CD-flower had a high sugar content. In their memory banks, each agent could recall the sweet experience associated with a certain CD, so when they encountered that CD again they would expect another sugary meal.

Instead of memories of fine music quality, the sugary rewards that became embedded in the agents' memories came from patterns exhibited in trends of upturned weekly sales, higher chart movements, and more frequent levels of airplay. It was the pattern of movement and change in these sensorial channels that attracted the agents' attention; it was the pattern of change that became part of their memories, and it was those early changes that turned the hits into hits that gave agents the rewards they sought.

When we first turned on our program, we found our agents rapidly diverging into two groups. The first group was composed of a small number of early-warning broadcasters that were quick to spread the word about changes in the patterns they were seeing in the sales and airplay trends. The second group was a much larger collection of followers that did not make a move to call a quickly rising CD a hit until it was nearly certain that indeed a hit was imminent. Once this was apparent, this group would simultaneously flock to discussing and producing a hit. In contrast, risk-seeking agents were the first movers who achieved a large portion of reward when they accurately called a trend very early in the cycle, while risk-averse agents typically tried to find a trend, were wrong, and settled back into a state that was similar to the fear of becoming embarrassed about being wrong again. Our agents were reacting and learning from their actions and mistakes.

These learning, bee-brained agents in our models were dissimilar from the more robotic network-software robots, or "bots," that are really a bunch of human-specified rules. Network-resident bots hold code to perform a certain action in a particular environment. For example, one bot application includes discovery of low-cost airline fares through website search and negotiation. But rule-driven automatons that search for websites have trouble learning about the experiences they encounter, and learning is fundamental to our agents' programs. Moreover, each of our agents is an independent calculator of the world it perceives; each has individual experiences and a pathway through simulated time that it alone encounters. How each agent arrives at a conclusion about where to place its decisions on a spectrum of risk taking is reminiscent of fashion, and the pace at which fashion evolves.

Fads and Fashions

Each of us wears an expression of our risk-taking preferences in the clothes we wear. The phrase "fashion forward" can help identify those fashion-conscious individuals who are not only highly aware of fashion trends but choose to purchase and exhibit a currently fashionable set of clothes as a signal of their awareness.

In the recorded-music industry, we found a number of identifiable fashion markers that people chose to adorn themselves with to identify themselves, such as Dave Matthews hats, Metallica T-shirts, and Grateful Dead ties. In the agent world, we put these markers on individual agents as so-called tags. These tags identify the preference of individual agents as belonging to a social group that can be recognized even without direct conversation from one agent to another. Fashion, like recorded music, afforded us another opportunity to analyze the social behavior of our agents as it pertains to hit making.

In August of 1996, we gathered up our Silicon Graphics machines and headed to present the first results of our Fads and Fashion program to a group of cognitive scientists, sociologists, and economists in Santa Fe. Of interest to these scientists was the social behavior of our agents, specifically how they created a social hierarchy spontaneously from a set of individuals that were connected by a random set of linkages we called a friends network. This was where the graphical power of the SGI was revealed, in portraying the individual actions of a society of agents. We were able to show through animation each agent's attitudes and how they changed each day of simulated time in 1995. Each agent was represented by a block of color that grew redder as it became more interested in a particular CD. Most important, we were able to graphically chart the outcome of their individual forecasts into an accurate prediction of the growth of the overall market for three albums of 1995, Hootie & the Blowfish, Seal, and a Rod Stewart release.

As the year went into springtime, we saw the colors of groups of individual agents shift from a variety of shades of pale yellow (indicating mild disinterest) to a very distinct tangerine, representing the similarity in outlook and zeal with which these individuals coherently promoted the virtues of Hootie & the Blowfish. The simulation's color shift turned into a hot crimson as the agents reached a fever pitch when, in the fall of 1995, they started listening to the single "Time," which went into heavy rotation on many radio stations around the country, and album sales took off. We were able to describe these groups of individuals as clear customer segments only for a period of a few weeks, at which time they dissipated again into a set of individuals with less clearly aligned thinking and biases. Segmentation of populations of consumers was more a dynamic phenomenon, not a clear cluster or permanent club. We saw agents start out in a cluster and become aligned in thinking about a particular product, only to migrate away when they became bored and distracted by another hot CD. While other agents can come in to replace the defectors, what was important in retaining a coherent market was control over the rate of individual migration into and out of the market, giving the illusion of a permanent customer segment.

In our artificial worlds, we could stop time for more than one agent snoozing against a tree, and put a whole community of agents to sleep. We are also able to thaw out these frozen agents in a slightly different world than the one they went to sleep in. While the agents sleep, we can grow thorns outside castle walls, and even change the laws of our agent's simulated physics. In many of our agent-built experiments, we freeze a particularly provocative population, say of moviegoers, and awaken them in another time to see what their reaction might be if their movie choices are completely changed. It's like freezing the line awaiting Hitchcock's 1960 opening of *Psycho*, and waking them up in 1999, to see if they would wait in line to see *The Blair Witch Project*.

What These "Natural Worlds" Can Teach

When I used to think of the art of giving advice, I'd recall the sequential steps of interview, analysis, and presentation. And in that presentation the logical production of a story would be woven, a compelling drama linking findings to distilled conclusions to refined recommendations.

Yet I now believe that this traditional advisory methodology can be augmented and joined to an approach that stems from complexity research, uses metaphors from nature, and is told as a conversation over time. This new method relies on repeated trials of computer-based experiments that derive findings as instances and examples from fully articulated artificial worlds.

Increasingly, advice needs to be delivered in near real time, as events occur. An advisor has to remain poised with a standing knowledge about how a client's business operates, and how the environment and competitive position are perceived. The advisor's role has evolved to spurring tactical actions that generate sustained hits, which, in turn, lead to an emergent strategic course.

As hits become an important component of value, fewer and fewer companies will have the patience to wait for their advisors to learn about the nuances of their companies, or about the particular crisis they may be facing at the time they are seeking advice. Companies require rapid response by skilled and seasoned practitioners as near-real-time advice becomes ever more valuable and volatile. The weeks spent in management interviews to discern perspectives and potential answers, followed by months of analytical research and study, followed by a formal presentation, can put advice out of date and out of touch with shifts in a dynamic market. Exponentially rising demand associated with hit markets do not allow considered, time-intensive advice. Instead, nonlinearity inspires an inductive, rapidly self-correcting advisory response that anticipates, observes, and learns.

In a hits-driven business, the volatility of advice becomes extreme—the value of that advice evaporates with the next market hiccup. Yet ongoing, aware, and attuned advisory capability retains its value. Unexpected events are placed into context, and that context is in turn updated with alternative courses of action and likely competitive countermeasures. Moreover, expected events are placed into that context, and these expectations reinforce the emergent schemata and rules that help the client make sense of the future as it becomes the present.

Automated advice is built from a suite of software tools that attempt to mimic the real world, but are contained in a simplified artificial world in a computer. Managers can react to changes in that artificial world, move forward or backward in time, and see how their decisions might play out. They can reflect how different their expectations were from how the world reacted. Their notion of fidelity to this world, however, changes over time. As you move deeply into the future and haze appears, there are a vast range of potential trajectories to get from today to all the possible tomorrows.

But before any of these real events took place, the same catalytic events can take place in a microcosm—an artificial world of silicon-based Lilliputians.

The night sleep thoroughly refreshed the owner of the real estate firm. A thought, clear as the Vermont air on a cool maple-sugaring morning, resonated in his head. I'll sell that parcel of land, he thought. What's one more after the two I sold a few months ago?

Two years later, Treewell had changed. As he suspected, the parcel of land he sold turned into an outlet store for one of those New York boutiques. Subsequently, the eighteenth-century blacksmith shop next door had been torn down and replaced with a gas station to accommodate all the tourists shopping at the new outlet stores. Development pressure in Treewell had become immense; the town was quickly losing the Treewellian character that it once had. Several longtime residents, in fact, had just moved out of the town, fed up with the insidious "Isn't that quaint, Harold?" and "Mom, doesn't this place have a

Gap?" comments that were now ubiquitously spewing forth from the mouths of the gawking tourists.

He could see the writing on the wall. It was only his minor, seemingly insignificant decisions to sell those parcels of land that had started the train down the slope that would change Treewell irrevocably. Indeed, even now, there was no going back—Treewell had become its own worst nightmare; its real history and charm was gone, replaced by fabricated narratives and imitation allure. Even he, once-proud resident of Treewell, was considering selling all his land that he had bought specifically so as to preserve it. The world changes, he thought sadly, by the small decisions we make every day.

5

WHERE HITS HAPPEN

SCENE: *The snobby Bushwood Country Club Golf Pro Shop, filled with the latest golfing merchandise of the highest quality and commensurate price, somewhere in Southern California.*

DRAMATIS PERSONAE

   Czervik *(Rodney Dangerfield)*
   Judge Smails *(Ted Knight)*
   Mr. Wang *(Dr. Dow)*

ACTION: *Dressed in a garish golfing outfit, Czervik and Wang enter the Bushwood pro shop like a whirlwind, looking around frantically, gesturing at the merchandise. Clearly mortified, shoppers, including Judge Smails, gasp at the sight of intruder Czervik.*

CZERVIK: Hey, orange balls! I'll have a box of those—and give me a box of those naked lady tees. *(Pointing at a particularly dreadful-looking hat on a rack in front of him)* This is the worst hat I've ever seen. You buy a hat like that, I bet you get a free bowl of soup.

He turns to see Judge Smails wearing that very hat, obviously pleased with his dapper look.

CZERVIK *(sarcastically)*: It looks good on you, though.

Czervik moves on, the whirlwind departs. Judge Smails quickly discards the offending hat.

—CADDYSHACK

Most of us can relate to Judge Smails's chagrin in this scene from *Caddyshack*. Sometimes in our own world, with the tacit approval of those around us, we wear fashions and behave in ways that others might find garish or even offensive. Within the boundaries of our little world, these actions feel perfectly rational. The calm nature of the pro shop before Czervik's arrival, for example, was one of self-reinforcing behavior that included purchasing and wearing hats, shoes, belts, and other garb that would be out of place anywhere but on a country-club golf course. It took an external observer with a new (and in this case offensive) opinion to shatter that mood. Embarrassed, Judge Smails discarded a hat that he had considered not just acceptable but even dapper because it had been publicly ridiculed—ironically, by the least dapper guy around.

Smails's behavior speaks to the message of this chapter— that fashion, which dictates hits, is created as a social phenomenon. One of the most powerful insights for managers is an understanding of the dynamics of fashion—how it is created, sustained, and destroyed. In so doing, managers can set the stage for hits to happen.

Over time, products and brands can generate an incumbency effect. Like political figures ready for reelection, they build upon an established identity in the public eye with all its associations, resulting in new models, feature-rich versions, and improved products. Companies introduce these iterations, variations, and reiterations over time to reinforce previously learned buying patterns that are burned into our reflexive actions. Sometimes as a tactical move, a competitor will try to disrupt one locked-in pattern and quickly reestablish another to its own advantage. In some industries with a fashion component, one metagame is to produce a set of disruptive actions that knocks the old fashion off and sets the stage for a new wave.

In this chapter, we look at how managers can shape their showrooms, stores, and retail outlets into environments where they can create and sustain lock-in for as long as it produces profitable actions. These dynamic environments can be modified to help motivate customers to talk about and buy products in a way that builds and reinforces excitement. Managers can use experiments to better understand how design changes in these environments will affect individuals and their transactions.

Within these environments, very specific social effects can dramatically alter the outcome of transactions by tipping the scale from one lock-in to another. A fleeting glance, a few words, or the exchange of a blue blouse for a pair of slacks is certainly no great interaction, but such things matter to consumers. Within these cauldrons, these actions are more than deliberated transactions, debated choices, and impulse purchases; the people involved in them are guided by the sometimes more-than-additive combination of advertisements, sales incentives, and peer pressure. Sometimes they are shocked into action. And predicting what, when, and where these people are likely to make their transactions can spell the difference between unsold stock and empty shelves waiting for replacement.

Standing Ovations

At some point we cease to be autonomous purchasing individuals and join the crowd. Think of a standing ovation, which represents one of the most basic and fundamental forms of emergent behavior. Whether we are reacting to a piece of unexpectedly beautiful oratory, or musical virtuosity, or a home run, we may wonder how a standing ovation gets started. Perhaps two or three individuals in the front row quickly stand up and start the reaction. But what if there were two or three people in the back row, or there was only one that stood up? The emergent phenomenon of an ovation either happens or it doesn't. Sometimes an ovation might get stuck halfway down a room, with clumps of people standing; other times it spreads like a wave, starting in some areas, fanning out until the whole arena is covered.

Students of the Computational Economics School in Santa Fe have built a series of computer models of standing ovations. Their challenge: to build a realistic, bottom-up exercise of how individuals communicate with one another to produce an emergent ovation. They factor in such variables as the size of the concert hall and the reverberation of sound pressure when the ovation's clapping reaches a threshold.

The standing-ovation analogy is germane to retail hits in a physical way. Think of the standing ovation as a wave in a confined space, this time an expanding wave of flame in a reaction chamber. We can think of the crowd combusting, or simultaneously reacting to the event, and then self-organizing the ovation. The level at which people become triggered to stand can be learned and passed along throughout the audience. The defining event (the end of a speech, or the pleasing crack of a well-hit home run) can be enough to fire individual triggers and catalyze enough early adopters quickly enough so that others can see those reactants, follow suit, and explode the entire ovation in a flash. With enough knowledge about what it takes to compel individuals to action, managers can determine what social environment can be generated to create a more expansive reaction from a crowd or a market.

Smart managers understand the importance of catalyzing an environment, or understanding when and how to apply an effective shock to the system. Just as bombs explode in a chain reaction, managers need to discover how to create shock waves that get the explosions we call hits to occur. A key part of this formula is determining how much energy will help guarantee a hit as a response. This calls for breaking out both the speed and the magnitude of the shock wave. The speed relates to how fast the shock wave will travel as it travels through a population. The magnitude of the wave signifies how large a shock it will take to change behaviors—how expensive it will be to deliver that level of shock.

And hits are about the buzz, the conversation that is bound into products as they become fashionable among a huge group of people at the same time.

Managing Expectations

Today, fashion and its attendant conversation are ever more embedded into everything we buy. Consider the role of styling in the historic evolution of the American automotive industry. By 1920, Ford Motor Company had built a commanding market position by developing the most efficient production system on the planet, resulting in the low-cost and populist Model T. In the mid-1920s, General Motors, led by Alfred Sloan, countered by introducing a set of cars differentiated mainly by superficial styling changes in body shape. In so doing, the company could offer special features that appealed to different segments of the growing market.

To keep up with the styling changes introduced by GM, Ford went through a costly (then $18 million) makeover of its production facilities to make the Model A, an entirely new car. Yet according to author David Gartman, in his book *Auto Opium*, Henry Ford still clung to his utilitarian philosophy of one standardized, unchanging motorcar for everyone, leading to an inflexible system. Ultimately, Ford's inability to build an adaptive production facility that could react to quick changes in the market's tastes spelled trouble for the company's industry leadership position.

Fast-forward to the 1950s, where Harley Earl's styling staff at GM became industry leaders through their unique sense of style. Styling set the pace of industry evolution. Among the players vying for market leadership and sales, a styling war erupted. The race was on for more and more extreme versions of the appealing appendages of sheet metal and chrome. In this styling war, casualties such as the Edsel would soon emerge, and extinctions would eventually sweep through the automotive industry. But at the height of style proliferation, in 1959, fins had become huge and differentiated to resemble strange shapes, including batwings and eyebrows. Even Chrysler's Virgil Exner, who introduced the fins, exclaimed that "It was obvious that I had given birth to a Frankenstein."

But it wasn't just the automobiles themselves that were undergoing radical changes in the late 1950s. It was also the coevolution of these cars with the self-image of the people buying those products. Increasingly, you *were* your car. This was a radical shift in self-image, and was linked to the simultaneous product proliferation that resulted from (and responded to) the burgeoning influence of television, which sparked a new, more intimate, and more persuasive style of personalizing and selling things.

People gained a profound attachment to new cultural artifacts such as automobiles, washing machines, even houses. Television programming and commercials helped induce the buying mood. Dinah Shore sang, "See the USA in your Chevrolet," and televised visions of the nascent interstate highway system inspired many families to pack their Fords for a trip across the country filled with memories of motel pools, national parks, and the family station wagon filled to maximum capacity.

Product proliferation extended to the places where products were sold. Dream showrooms of the 1950s shaped the seminal point at which the transactions were made, where people could attach themselves through these products to the dreams that these products could fulfill. The role that these showrooms played in product display was critical to the development of the style-conscious society of the times.

Not long ago, people could ride in their dream-fulfilling cruisers, the desperately desirable, fin-draped cars. And they wanted to go to a place where they could reinforce their desire for those dream makers. They wanted to return to the retail showroom when the real-world reality of their existing cars' squeaks, rattles, and rust spots no longer matched their expectations as portrayed in the new commercials they were shown. Like flowers that attract bees with a reliable quantity of satisfying sugar, the retail showroom presented a promise of reliable rewards, and products sold there tried to heighten customers' expectations of the future.

Today those reward expectations evolve so rapidly that the pace of change exceeds the rate at which some retail product display locations can be modified. Henry Ford produced an efficient Model T production system that was built for a pace of society where function alone was fulfilled at a market-expanding low price. By the 1950s, when the pace of product change had exceeded a critical rate, fashion had converged and in many cases usurped function. Long-standing marquee models such as Studebakers and Ramblers fell by the wayside as the tastes of consumers became more fickle and, as it were, fleeting.

Today the rapid waves of demand in the market have forced retailing systems to develop ever more efficient ways of meeting demand. Today's hits press inventory management to the limit of its calculus. It seems fitting that the Four Seasons restaurant in New York occupies the site of a former showroom that catalyzed dreams in the 1950s; enduring classics have given way to changing daily menus. Despite (perhaps because of) today's quicker metabolism, the role of retail locations—the containers in which these explosions happen—remains critical to keep us focused on matching people's expectations directly to the things that will make our retail dreams come true.

Memes and Markets

Few consumers act alone when deciding what to buy. When we share the emotions of choosing a car, or a movie, we are replicating our view of what we want our world to look like. We pass a meme along to others. Just what is a meme? In his book *At Home in the Universe*, Stuart Kauffman writes:

> Richard Dawkins, an evolutionary biologist at Oxford, popularized the word "meme." In the simplest image, a meme is a bit of behavior that is replicated in a population. Women now wear sunglasses perched on the top of their heads. I suspect that this was spawned by Audrey Hepburn playing Holly Golightly in the movie *Breakfast at Tiffany's* many years ago. In this limited sense, memes are "replicators" which are invented and then imitated in complex patterns of cultural transmission.

Meme passing is a way to create a sort of "organic chemistry" between people. Strike up a conversation. What's to talk about? You search for a common bond. The common interest may be a restaurant or a hot fashion designer; talking about it connects you. Then, like modems seeking the right level, you constantly adjust up, looking for a more robust connection.

Conversation, which links people through meme transmission, is fundamental to why we buy, and why we want to buy what others are buying. It's at the heart of why there's a Top 40 rock singles chart, for instance, or a buzz around the Toyota Camry "beating" the Ford Taurus for the top automobile of 1997. Every week the newspapers dutifully report the weekend box-office performance of the top films. Do people really care about the fortunes of Hollywood studios? No. They read these listings as faithfully as a box score because they care about what other people care about. They want to know what everyone else knows and is seeing, and what, then, they might like.

A meme can be a personal fashion statement as simple as liking the looks of a car or the smell of a brand of soap. And the transmission of memes can be understood by drawing from chemistry, where a higher level of organization between atoms displays a new and different form of behavior. Similarly, as people (comprising molecules) buy products as a group, we start out with a set of rules about our behavior and end up with an entirely different set. Our behavior as individuals purchasing a car might be very different from the behavior we exhibit as individuals buying soap. And how we form our opinions may not be random, but part of an orchestrated chemical reaction in a constrained environment, or a crucible. A crucible can simply be the retail environment we find ourselves in, which puts us in a higher state of buying excitement. Within that crucible, we can find the right catalysts in the form of salespeople and internally generated "heat" that help to get us over our resistance to purchasing.

Markets emerge and persist, like a standing wave of an ice-crystal-filled cloud over Everest's mountaintop. The myriad decisions that make up a changing market are like countless accreting snowflakes compressing onto one another in a more solid waveform. Markets can move glacially, changing form with only the most persistent or unusual of displacements.

Markets persist too, for decades and longer, even though the individual choices that combine, coalesce, amplify, and get them flowing in one direction have long evaporated. While some early experiments flutter and die out, those that last must have a defining quality that can be revealed in retrospect. The character of these markets can last far into the future; we can expect that these markets will help shape decisions that will in turn shape the formation of the persistence of yet another market. The legacy of individual choices made long ago is hard to alter.

Take, for example, the great American standard, the Buick. The feeling of the Buick automobile has stood longer than the actual styling and motor train of each new year's model introduction. Consumers of those new year models change year after year. And so do the Buicks. It is not surprising that most cars end up rusting away, after being passed from owner to owner until they are no longer repaired or are damaged beyond reasonable repair. They succumb to the eventual pull of iron and chromium turning to dust. Those relics that hang on in the sunny climes of rust-free California can serve as the restored classics and antique license-plate holders twenty-five years or more after they are made. But each of these preserved or restored examples is rare, as their nostalgic but escalating prices reflect in the used car market.

Perhaps less well known is the similar fleeting presence of the buyers in the market. Physicists will tell us that as human beings, we too last for only a couple of years or so; in that time all of our individual atoms have come and gone, and many of our cells have also come and gone, although some remain. Yet we too persist as a standing wave of a thinking, breathing organism capable of buying Buicks, if we can and choose to.

I will never forget the series of white Buicks that my grandfather bought in the 1960s, one of which I eventually drove as my first car as a teenager. The comfortable ride, smooth feel, and wide hood expanse were buttressed by the immense feeling of 400-cubic-inch power under the hood and a silky undercurrent of an automatic transmission underneath the floorboards. Yet I'm not the same person I once was. Now with a family, and past some of my middle-age crisis, I've been through cars that ranged from pickup trucks and behemoth station wagons to turbo-powered sports cars, far from the Buick feel of decades ago.

But the market for Buicks has persisted from my grandfather's day. Managing that market of producing and selling Buicks may be like sailing a huge supertanker through a turbulent ocean: There's a lot of momentum there, but turning can come only with great expense and vigor. But even a supertanker analogy leaves me short of the actual sense of indirect control over the demand-management skills required. The thousands of dealers, buyers, cars, repair parts, advertisements, and sales incentives have to be managed constantly. And yet changes to those individual parts, like the myriad interlocking ice crystals, function within a set of boundaries that are somewhat glacial. The demography of the buyers stays roughly in place; the neighborhood character of the dealerships may change, but slowly; and each year's new model still gives the comfortable cruising ride and noise-free smoothness of quality.

The real job may be to hold everything together as the markets move ahead in time. Adjusting this, tweaking that, careful not to experiment too much for fear of shattering the market that has coevolved from the interactions among buyers and dealers. Like a beautiful gem in the midst of being cut into an even more beautiful piece of jewelry, the changes to the market must be precise and considered; the danger of destruction is very real. Early experimental decisions about product positioning and buyer characteristics are made; later decisions can serve as corrective moves.

Consider the purchase of a family car. In this instance, a leading brand of Detroit-made automobile attempts to find the likely buyers of that model and persuade prospects to eventually buy—or maybe lease. Today's automobile market in the U.S. is filled with sales incentives that trade off purchase discounts with attractively priced leasing options. Prices for new cars remain high, but there is a quiet discount war raging. Every year, the media like to keep tabs on the most popular automobile in the United States. In 1997 Toyota Camry stole the crown from Ford Taurus, which had held the top spot for five years. But at what cost? Sales incentives are expensive, and for an entire brand they can run into the billions per year. And yet there are predictive patterns of behavior among car companies. Some, like Ford, typically accelerate the aggressiveness of their lease programs as the model year winds down. Toyota spends more on cash incentives and offers modest leases only briefly. And these sale incentives are not the whole story—there are also innumerable sales contests, dealer incentives, cooperative advertising programs, and race team sponsorships.

Taken from the manufacturer's point of view, there may be

reasons to increase financial incentives if styling or available features place a car in a disadvantageous position. Consider what happened when the Taurus introduced a dramatic new body shape in the 1995 model year. To keep Taurus as the most popular brand, aggressive leases were added that year. But taken from the dealer's perspective, the day's inventory supply adds carrying costs to the dealers' incentives from the factory. Thus, the dealer may be oriented to remove costly inventory instead of selling the most popular model. The dealer is an active observer of the local market, and adapts according to what is wanted and what will be most profitable. As an economic agent, a dealer learns over time what the factory will do with the cars on the lot as the model year ends, and also learns what the competitors, other manufacturers and dealers, are likely to do. This learned behavior becomes expected after a time, and in some cases, a part of what dealers do. But the learning doesn't end at the dealer level, it extends to the customers themselves, and can produce a learned behavior, expectation, that is locked in on a profit-destroying pathway.

Fashion and Cocktail Parties

What is fashion? Who defines it? Why is it that some trends tend to sweep across the country and take a firm hold whereas others are short-lived and die quickly? These are questions that people have been trying to answer since designers have been trying to sell clothing. It is a difficult topic to quantify because there is no one true answer. But at PricewaterhouseCoopers, we have tried to understand the waves of fashion and its methods of spreading. My colleague Anita Shieh studies fashions and finds them to be varied, nonlinear, and oftentimes specific to an individual event. Where fashion is concerned, people make decisions not as true individuals, but not as true groups either. Their decision to adopt and therefore buy a certain style, although it may be an individual act, is influenced and shaped by a number of different forces, which may or may not conspicuously affect the individual. These forces may span demographic issues, such as geography and race, as well as more subjective issues such as advertising, peer influences, and the media. Obviously, these influences affect different people in a number of different ways, creating a vast spectrum of clothing styles offered to the public.

People obviously do not make fashion-type decisions as a group, because otherwise, everybody would be embracing the same styles—we all would be wearing the same type of clothing. At the same time, we are not exactly individualistic either, no matter what we would personally like to believe. As a result, our individual decisions are made up of a number of subgroups. Each group has different standards for what is considered in vogue. Consequently, each person in the group is influenced by the fashion decisions of others in the same group. Fashion-forwardness or fashion-consciousness as a whole, then, is completely relative and changes depending on the context in which it is being used. Even the punk rockers who dye their hair green, blue, or purple have mohawks, and wear their tattered, duct-taped clothing with metal studs and chains are considered fashionable in their own group because that is the standard.

Every once in a while, an individual in a group may become a fashion innovator by introducing a new style, form of clothing, or way of wearing clothing into his group. Whether this new item eventually becomes adopted or fails depends upon a number of factors, including wearability and/or the popularity of the individual. If this person is looked up to as a "fashionable person," or has already been established as a fashion innovator, chances are that that particular look will be integrated into the group and accepted as their own.

Take, for example, the relatively recent trend of wearing thrift-shop clothing. While such clothes were always considered fashionable by many people, the fact that models and fashion designers have begun wearing them has exposed the idea to people who perhaps would never have thought to wear such clothes. In fact, fashion designers, models, and movie stars instigate a number of popular fashion trends. The result is a trickle-down effect wherein those who have closest access to the star and consider themselves part of that particular fashion group adopt the fashion in its purest form.

This, however, is not the only way in which fashion trends run through the population. Take, for example, the grunge look that was so popular in the early nineties. It's no accident that tattered jeans and flannel shirts grew popular with the rise in popularity of grunge music out of Seattle. As this style of clothing caught on, even high-end fashion designers began incorporating the look into their own collections, spreading the trend to groups of people who perhaps would never have worn such a style. The same happened with the designer Tommy Hilfiger. He took a style that was popular on the streets and incorporated it into his designs. Today we have at least two types of Hilfiger-influenced fashion cultures, the suburban prep and urban prep look. The prominent Hilfiger logo and color choices give an aura of prestige to wearers in each distinct group.

If one person is wearing a particular style and is seen by others who happen to like the way he looks, the imitators will make an effort to incorporate that look into their own wardrobes. Consequently, others see them and are affected by them in a chain reaction. These interactions can take place at parties, churches, bars, luncheons—wherever people gather together in a group. If you observe a group closely, you will find that the people within it tend to dress very similarly. It is as if the group itself or the environment somehow defines the standard of clothing. If you go into a trendy bar in New York City, you can expect the majority of the people to be wearing black.

When one person introduces a new style into a group, thereby upsetting an equilibrium, it is up to the members of the group to accept or reject it. If everyone dislikes it, the person who introduced the style will be thought of as unfashionable. If everyone likes it, they might be motivated to incorporate the style into their own wardrobes and consider that person fashion-forward. Finally, if a few people like the style, it becomes dependent on the popularity of the people who like it as to whether or not the style spreads through the group.

There are a number of different ways to use this cycle of fashion to our advantage as businesspeople. Small boutique-type stores tend to preselect a particular group to sell their products to. This is due to the size constraint of these stores—the fact that they cannot supply many different styles to a number of different people. Thus, they cater to a certain group or groups of consumer and design their retail environment accordingly. Larger, department-type stores, however, must provide an environment that will cater to the needs of a diverse group of people. Department stores may do so by creating different moods and scenes to attract consumers to different areas of the store. For example, the department that houses designer women's fashion has a totally different ambiance than that of juniors' clothing. Each area is designed to attract the target consumer to that area and make her feel more comfortable. So, while the designer women's clothing area may be more elegant, and outfitted with comfortable, plush sofas and jazz or classical music, the juniors' area features neon lights and either rock music or rock videos on monitors. These kinds of visual and auditory displays naturally help filter customers and direct them toward the kinds of products they want to purchase. Another visual filter is the mannequins in each area. Often a consumer who is just browsing with no real intention to buy will see an attractive outfit displayed on a mannequin and will enter the actual selling area to see what else is offered there. While customers may not always have a specific idea in their minds as to what they want to buy when going shopping, they usually have a certain idea of the styles of clothing that appeal to them and naturally gravitate toward these.

By building a more adaptive system, it is possible that retail stores may be able to target a wider base of consumers. Instead of specifically targeting small groups of shoppers for different styles of clothing, there may be a way to find a more universal environment or way to display the good offered. Although it is difficult to build an adaptive retail store, since items would have to be physically moved back and forth, it is possible for Internet shopping. By changing the environment and even goods offered according to a person's personal tastes, retail stores may have a better chance at turning a browser into a buyer.

Mining Data for Insight

How can we best understand this retail environment? One of the best ways is to gather transaction data and analyze it. Managers catalyze retail environments through subtle changes based on insights garnered simply from reading data. We aren't surprised to see everything bar-coded these days, and aren't fazed by the routine use of ruby-red laser light taking account of our purchases in the checkout line. Where this scanner data goes, of course, is into a series of computers, where it's collected and calibrated to produce a running tab on inventory levels and unit sales. Then where does this data go? Eventually, it probably gets thrown away.

For most companies, like Sainsbury's, one of the largest grocery chains in the U.K., there is simply too much data to make use of. It just gets collected and used for a short while for near-term demand forecasting, stored for a few months, and then tossed. Where are all the historic patterns of purchasing habits? For most companies, gone with the wind. But a new, more efficient discipline is emerging, which is fast becoming popular in the new consulting vernacular—data mining. For the most part, this new technique involves the use of computers to measure and evaluate marketing and operations data. Data-mining computers can find patterns that would have taken human analysts inordinate amounts of time to sift through. The computer can also find correlations between sales of Victoria's Secret green push-up bras and sales of Victoria's Secret CDs that are sold at the checkout counter. Market-basket studies, including bras, CDs, and other consumer products, are the main focus of many data-mining efforts.

Sainsbury's has another exciting application of data mining: customer-loyalty cards. The company has seen an explosive growth in this new tool. When the purchases of items on these cards are tallied and mined, the company can tabulate trends of individual buying patterns. These series can include how frequently a single customer makes particular purchases, and whether an in-store coupon may have motivated the purchase or caused the customer to purchase a competing brand. While market-basket studies are still performed, these studies can now become correlated over a longer time frame than just a single purchase date, encompassing a single customer's purchasing behavior over months or even years.

Managing customer loyalty is one of the hottest trends of retailing today, and the use of computer-assisted data mining to discern time series trends is critical to finding loyalty patterns. But a problem remains. There are thousands, even millions of patterns that a computer can find interesting that can be displayed to the final arbitrator of relevance, the human decision maker. This is where data visualization comes in. Computer-aided visualization started in scientific distillation of millions of observations into something that makes sense and is appealing. As one of the main drivers of this quest for greater and greater computing power, visualization allows pictures of phenomena to be portrayed on computer screens. The quest for greater fidelity, higher resolution, and the use of three dimensions is just a start. Add time series animations to that three-dimensional space and the ability to fly through time and space interactively, to change perspectives on a whim and a push of the button. Portraying the dynamics of consumer demand also requires the use of vast computing power. Visualization of individual behavior is a challenge, but seeing the simultaneous actions of thousands of individuals, and making sense out of what their behavior means, is an even greater challenge.

There has always been a love affair between market research and the computer, and that relationship has grown even more prominent. Consider the fascinating simulation that has been built by Professor Raymond R. Burke at Indiana University, which I visited recently. Without leaving the laboratory, I worked my way down virtual aisles of shelves stocked with frozen peas and other sumptuous vegetables. With my data gloves, I moved these items into my cyber-shopping basket, pointed to the checkout port, and arranged for home delivery.

There is something to the traditional store layouts that may have little to do with cultural perspectives, and more to do with lock-in—"the way we've always done it." At Sainsbury's the layout of a store follows a traditional pattern, with a grid of aisles at ninety degrees, to allow stocking and shopping convenience. In a smaller store, the choice of brands that are made available and the product categories, such as coffee, dairy, and crackers, are displayed in different areas of the store. But if these component products were part of a project purchase, say for an afternoon tea, the shopper would likely pass by one area, go to another, and then find his way to the third. With a more comprehensive shopping agenda, the customer would likely

travel up one aisle and down another, remembering each project, like a particularly requested breakfast treat for the children, a week's worth of dinners, and adding that one spice that
is naggingly absent from the shelves. Managers can thus
achieve a form of customer lock-in, where the individual shoppers feel that rather than going through the motions of shopping robotically, they are actively engaged, being delighted by
the store's novelty and surprise.

Aventuras in Baby Strollers

To determine how we can start to understand how to shape
environments that create lock-in, and the hits that come and
go, we have to look at how retail sales happen—how to simulate history as well as forecast the future.

On June 16, it was another hot and sultry day in Miami,
and customers flocked in to see the bargains in the Macy's
Aventura store. Every cash register was hooked on-line, recording each transaction, and time-stamping the sale with the customer's use of credit card or cash for the purchase. Macy's
typically captures this data for analytical purposes; we've been
able to help with an innovative new use for it. By using this
data as the demographic basis for synthetic customers, we can
play these transactions back digitally, as artificial customers
and employees manning the store. In a setting reminiscent of
Bill Murray in the movie *Groundhog Day*, Macy's can experiment
with multiple outcomes of the Aventura store until it optimizes
traffic flow. Or Macy's management can put a greater number
of employees into the jewelry department to see how the cus-

WHERE HITS HAPPEN   151

tomers, albeit artificial, like the level of service and attention. They can try out a design for the store that moves the profitable cosmetics section, grow it to a larger footprint, and add more space for new lines of fragrances that may be big sellers.

Not long ago, Bill Connell, vice president for Macy's East Operations, was determined to find a way to modernize his model of retail operations. He had built a model with spreadsheets about ten years ago that was still in use and still useful. But Bill sensed that this spreadsheet model missed something critical. It didn't capture the dynamic essence of the ups and downs of retailing. On a sale day, and there are many at Macy's, many more customers came in to take advantage of advertised bargains. He wondered how the store should be staffed on those sale days compared to a normal business day. He used rules of thumb, but they were mostly averages, and ancient in origin. They had been developed years before, and perhaps did not even apply to the business conditions in the Miami geography, or with the demography of Aventura shoppers, or the consuming climate of the late 1990s. How could he tell if the current store's operating plan had anything close to an optimal number of employees staffing the store at these peak times?

Bill decided to try agent-based simulation to look at the store's health and expected profits under a range of conditions. He could turn the real-life Aventura into an experimental store with an entire suite of alternatives, but if he changed that solitary store he'd have no control variable, no frame of reference against which to evaluate how well the experiment worked. But computer-based simulation offered an approach to test literally thousands of scenarios and setups to see which one was best. Even more important, the simulation could self-organize and try out alternatives on its own without Bill even considering them.

Many business managers with operational responsibilities like Bill Connell use variance analysis to determine causes of failures and unexpected windfalls. Historical actual sales, revenues, and operating statistics are used to develop benchmarks for future comparison. This single trail of what-actually-did-happen versus what-could-have-happened is the fodder for data-mining techniques. And the patterns of that single trail that were missed or forgotten by humans can be mined in more detail by computer software. Enter computer simulation, where possible historical patterns can be discovered by humans and by mining techniques.

One possible first step in building a computer simulation for a retail environment like Aventura is to look at the store from the customers' and employees' points of view. Whether the environment performs at a maximum level depends on what these individuals can accomplish. If the actions of the customers match their shopping goals, we've met one criterion. And if the employee effectively delivers the service that encourages the customers to purchase, we have yet another positive meter reading. The actions and reactions of these individual customers and employees have to be encoded into their potential repertoire of behaviors. And another thing—emotions, however rudimentary and crude, must be considered, as customers inevitably have affinities toward certain departments and goods, and feel good about the store when they can find what they are looking for. In simulations built from the bottom up, customers and employees as agents each have a set of rules about what they would do if they encountered particular situations, and have a set of affective, emotional states that correspond to the fulfillment of their goals. But whether these rules are invoked, and whether these goals are reached, depends on the local conditions that surround each individual agent.

One critical test of this simulated environment is to see whether the actions of the agents in the virtual space matches the historical reality. This process begins with each agent acting as a customer with ingrained habits, required to conduct transactions at exactly the same time they took place historically. We can start to infer the demography of customers and even learn about their historic purchase patterns. But we know nothing about the people who just came into the store to browse, or those who came in and then left without completing the transaction they wanted to. In addition, we have computer agents that get smart—maybe not as smart as humans, but smart enough. So while it may be simpler to replicate and analyze historic actions in a store, you'll see a whole lot more if you consider the myriad possible actions that could have been taken by *all* of the individuals in the store on the day the actual transactions were conducted.

Much has been written in the computer science literature about the relative ease in which complex behaviors can arise from the actions of autonomous agents, each with a set of simple rules and a restricted number of possible behaviors. But practitioners will quickly agree that the rich behavior, or "complexity for free," as it is sometimes called, paradoxically comes at a cost. First, the amount of required testing that turns the possible set of actions into a plausible set of actions that mimics the real world can be enormous. Second, the set of actions that agents take that leads to the mimicked behavior may have little to do with the actual actions that gave rise to that real behavior in the real world. We can ask, "Did the customer buy the jewelry because she loved it or was it the last item in the case that fit the need?" But the third cost is one that is both the most important and the most ephemeral: How can we build a simulation that we can trust to tell us anything about the world in which we live? This notion of trust is usually wrapped in an aura of accuracy—how accurately we can portray historic actions, and whether simulations tuned to behave like the historic past can tell us much about alternative futures.

Hits Over Time

Such lessons from simulations can help managers create and sustain hits over time, and in such a manner that their profitability is more than random. They do so by recognizing how hits persist.

People profit from the single hit—the *Titanic*, the Hootie, the Ernie. There will never be another movie like *Titanic*, or a rock group like Hootie & the Blowfish, or a doll just like Elmo. And we wouldn't want them again. Their special qualities remain, but their specialness is gone, a part of history. It's because their specialness is human history, reflected in the first reactions of consumers to special effects, warm melodies, cute giggles. And even if there were new *Titanic*s, Hooties, and Elmos, they would be imitators, shunned for their lack of originality and creativity.

But the original hits could not and would not have been hits without the environment into which they were introduced and then shaped. It's the environmental modeling that's of value to managers, as valuable as the search for the hit. It's not just the hit's intrinsic value, measured in cinematic prowess, musical virtuosity, or surprising play, but how each hit affects the environment into which it's released. Management decisions that contemplate knowing what will happen when a hit does indeed occur can steer a company toward profit.

If a potential hit comes along and is not nurtured, it will flash and burn out. But can the hit maker learn from a successful experience and attempt to replicate it? It was more than a product of randomness, of casting a wide enough net that the desperately few randomly huge hits were among the multiple fish caught. There are probably those who say we cannot predict when and where hits will happen, that success is cyclical.

I'm in the camp that believes we make our luck. Think of Hootie's success. When the first album burst onto the Top 40 scene, there was already in place, below the range of the national radar, a fanatic group of fans who had bought the group's self-released CDs. Maybe the group seemingly burst into our national consciousness, but it had been gathering momentum in the subconscious of many for some time. If there is only one Hootie, then the needle in the haystack has been discovered.

Let's suppose that musical groups explore every possible musical combination, variation, and innovation. With every departure from the norm, there is a random chance that one group will find the combination of new chords and melodies to become popular. Thus it is management's job to react quickly, jump on the groups that gain the strongest audience reactions, and sign them up before anyone else who is scouting for new sounds. This is where what one player expects to happen can actually influence the actions of others, and influence the outcome. If reggae starts to take off outside the urban centers of New York and Miami, a land rush can begin.

Finding that needle in a haystack sounds a little sad, like randomness ruling out anything more than a lucky discovery. Profits would then accrue only to those with the widest searches, or to those in the right place at the right time. Continuous profit making through any search strategy that does not take into account a full range of random possibilities would be impossible. To make a stream of cash flow with only luck at your side, you've got to be everywhere at once.

Once a hit happens, it changes the landscape of the marketplace forever. All subsequent hits will be informed by and somehow related to the success of previous products, and will begin to form their patterns, to spin their networks of fans, from the ground that has already sprouted such white-hot armies of fans as those of Hootie or Tickle Me Elmo. Ensuring success over the long term involves more than simply setting the stage for one hit. It involves looking for novel patterns within the entire environment in which hits happen, monitoring how the environment is changing as it is changing, and then always seeking lock-in from reality, not just a wish or a sense of nostalgia.

6

HITS FACTORIES

I hustled up Fifth Avenue in New York to finally arrive at the FAO Schwarz store, where in about an hour the Bandai hit toys called Tamagotchis were going to be sold in the United States for the first time. The line at the front door was orderly, given the press crews milling about, the garishly painted panel truck extolling the Tamagotchi's birth that was revolving around the block, and the human-inhabited plush-covered Tamagotchi waving at all the passersby. I made my way past about three hundred patiently waiting fans of the virtual pet, most of whom owing to their active conversation appeared to be natives of Japan, where the toy had become a national obsession, sold out whenever made available.

The Tamagotchi is one of the first examples of artificial life built for the mass public as entertainment. Artificial life was developed only several years ago, and was found only in a few computer games outside of academic labs and computer science departments. This nascent science had turned artificial intelligence on its ear, literally looking to build software-constructed life forms in a silicon computer. But instead of building expert systems that mimicked human thought from the onset, these artificial creatures learned from their experiences. They had genetic inheritance worthy of Mendel's peas, enjoyed a form of intercourse, propagation, and death, and sometimes took on compelling personalities. The Tamagotchis I was about to personally witness were affective, that is, given to expressing emotions, however primitive. They had evolved far from their origins in the labs of computer science departments a few years earlier.

Since I had met artificial-life guru and originator Chris Langton, we had spent many wonderful days and evenings together talking about what artificial life could evolve into. While Tamagotchis had begun to roam the earth, Chris was building an ambitious general construct for artificial-life experiments, called Swarm. We had also begun to build a series of artificial-life environments for business applications; while less general than Swarm, our tools were aimed at modeling hit businesses like the Tamagotchi being born this sunny day in New York.

I was on a mission. My two daughters, who clicked onto the Tamagotchi website from Japan, were keen to "be the first on their block" to own these new pets. They were already familiar with the quirks, the demands, and even the mortality of these digital creatures, and they had given me the sternest orders to secure one for each of them the day they appeared on the shelves. When I tried to explain that these toys might sell out before I could get them, they strongly urged me to try my best.

And so as I stood in line, motionless for about fifteen minutes or so, I happened to look inside the windows and see Barbie, another classic hit, an evergreen product that, like me, was a child of the fifties. Barbie had recently taken on more humanlike proportions. There were examples of her tucked into drawers and shelves all over my house, scores of them belonging to my daughters, who had since moved on to other passions. Barbie must have crowded out other competing fashion dolls for decades. Since her start in some distant past, Mattel had kept the fires burning with new extensions and introductions of friends, sisters, and boyfriends, houses and cars. Of course the Barbies I knew were mute: Whatever emotions they had were imbued into them at the time of play and the roles they had in fantasy.

Tamagotchis, on the other hand, beeped noisily when they wanted attention, and displayed happiness when cared for and anger when ignored. They needed care of their digital poop, and required nourishment in the form of binary snacks and meals. They required constant care while they were awake during their daytimes; while they slept, their human owners could get a few winks. And they progressed in age, as their images suggested, from newborn to adolescent to adult. And they died of old age, while Barbie was young forever. On the Tamagotchi web page my daughters frequented, they even found a Shinto priest icon beating drums for the souls of departed spirits of Tamagotchis that had passed on.

I was witnessing an artificial-life toy as a hit, characterized by the social buying frenzy that occurred when real-life group dynamics encountered this playful form of artificial intelligence. Bandai had manufactured the frenzy as well as the toy. The staging and orchestration of the launch was live before me, and echoed on CNN that afternoon. Bandai had learned from its experiences in Japan and Asia and was transferring that experience to building the market in the United States. Its first point of entry was here where I was standing among the first movers, the fans who would stoke the fires of demand. I could watch the emergence of a market from its first moments. It was too good to pass up the experience.

I braved the line, and was granted the allotment of two prized toys. Peace would reign in our household. Then I noticed that some of the recipients were happier than others. Those who received clear blue ones, in fact, seemed most thrilled. Mine were purple and yellow. Good enough, I thought, but the blue would be even better. I guessed that they were particularly rare and therefore even more desirable and cherished. If I was a really good father, I would get blue Tamagotchis. What to do? I got back in line.

I did get two more, a white and another yellow one. Exchanging them was out of the question. Nonetheless, all was well when I handed my prize booty to my daughters. And yet despite my apparent success, I wasn't satisfied. Getting shut out of the rarest of prizes, the blue clear plastic toy, hung heavy in my mind. If this blue talisman was rare, and if I could get it, then how much cooler, how much better that would be. Certainly my daughters would be the envy of other Tamagotchi-craving girls. I thought back to the coolness of the postage stamp printed upside down on its special page in my collection book (which I never obtained) or the double-stamped Lincoln pennies (one of which I found in my grandfather's change). Perhaps their satisfaction could compensate for the fad products I still longed to own—the exotic Ferrari sports car, red of course, or at least the Eddie Bauer edition sport utility Explorer. I admitted to myself that like others, I *wanted to join the club, to be admired and envied for owning the coolest new artifact.*

The weekends came and went. My daughters dutifully fed the digital pets, played with them, and even cleaned up after they pooped. And then one Monday afternoon I got a call from my sobbing daughter. She had forgotten to take her Tamagotchi to school and it had died, literally flown to heaven on the display screen. For more than an hour she was inconsolable. The emotional high of winning the lottery had been wiped out by the tears streaming down her cheeks. The affective computer had been successful, and devastating.

Becoming part of the Tamagotchi frenzy, getting caught up vicariously in the craze through my daughters, marked an eerie convergence of my work and life. I had already been thinking about how hits happen, and was using computers to help detect the patterns in real time, or real life, if you like. I had learned that in order to build good forecasting tools, you need agents that are emotionally reactive. Yet this was the first case I had seen where the things that were hits actually *were* artificial life. This experience reinforced for me the power of popular hits, which, when they come crashing through culture like a tidal wave, are exciting and all-encompassing.

Achieving "Lock-In"

What Tamagotchis show is that managers can systematically create and manage hits through a series of strategic decisions.

By identifying and then pushing or pulling the right strategic levers, managers can achieve a "lock-in" of consumers that tilts the emerging rules of competition toward their favor as the hit unfolds. This hit can then monopolize the hearts and minds of consumers. This chapter looks at how that happens.

In a recent *New Yorker* article, writer John Cassidy applied increasing-returns theory to Microsoft's market dominance, asserting:

> Microsoft's power comes from its ability to exploit what economists call "network externalities." ([Brian] Arthur uses the phrase "increasing returns," but he is talking about the same thing.) In plain English, "network externalities" means that the value of a product increases along with the number of other people who are already using it. This is not generally true—few people care how many others are buying the same brand of soap or cornflakes—but it usually applies to high-tech goods, for two reasons: they have to be compatible with one another (a Betamax videocassette player is of no use these days, because it can't play VHS cassettes), and they are often linked in a network, in which case the more people there are on the network the more valuable the product becomes. (A telephone is worthless if you're the only person who owns one.)

This paragraph contains a simple assumption with which I take issue: I believe that lock-in is not limited to high-tech markets, but that it takes place in any industry where ego is bound into the product. In fact, great managers and companies that could be deemed "hits factories" ensure a steady stream of hits over time by creating such lock-in through the dynamics of social behavior and consumer patterns. For these surfers of the waves of demand in the marketplace, social networks effectively become the ephemeral and flickering transmitter through which explosions transpire.

In entertainment, media, branded products—anywhere that ego is tied up with the product—social networks form that display such lock-in of emotional increasing returns. They become an intellectual and emotional monopoly, as it were, stealing the hearts and minds of many consumers at once, effectively dominating the conversation and locking out any meaningful competitors.

Though the mechanisms by which lock-in occurs are neither cast in silicon like MS-DOS, nor are they physical standards that help VHS videocassettes to knock Beta into market death, they are nonetheless as powerful and inexorable. Whenever consumers ask such questions as "How much do I care about being seen in my Jerry Garcia ties or in my Jeep?" or "Will cornflakes make me cool?" or "How popular will being the first to thump the pulpit for *The Blair Witch Project* make me among my friends?" they are ensuring the lock-in of a hit. While these links may lack the direct involvement of two users on a network, they nonetheless share the indirect involvement of conversation stoked through advertising, word of mouth, or any other product. These hits differ from the conventional model of technological lock-in in that they have a different metabolism. Lock-in occurs not on the time scale of an operating system, but much quicker.

Titanic's Tsunami

Consider the wild success of the motion picture *Titanic*, which in March 1998 became the highest-grossing film ever, with a combined domestic and international box office of more than $1 billion. According to Fox officials, in one Swiss town the number of tickets sold exceeded the town's population; in Spain, after a huge opening weekend, the second weekend was even bigger—surpassing any other first-weekend opening in Spain, ever.

And its success comprised more than mere box-office numbers; it won Golden Globe Awards and was nominated for and won eleven Oscars®. The buzz from the film was sufficient to spawn a slew of related hits: the film's soundtrack soared to the top of the charts, selling at the astonishing clip of 655,000 copies in the week following the picture's opening. The number two album, *Let's Talk About Love*, by Celine Dion, which that week sold 257,000, also carried the hit song "My Heart Will Go On" from the movie. And the book *James Cameron's Titanic* about the making of the film topped the *New York Times* nonfiction bestseller list. Even J. Peterman, the specialty catalog company, sold out its entire stock of *Titanic* props, including a lifeboat at $25,000.

The three-hour epic did not merely lock in its success through capturing mind share and heart share of moviegoers. By so dominating movie choices (more than one out of five viewers during the month of January was seeing the film for the second—or third—time) the epic effectively locked out the success of others.

This spectacular success surprised even the most optimistic of movie veterans. After the huge debacle of Kevin Costner's *Waterworld* (whose domestic box office of $88 million fell short of its estimated $170 million production costs), conventional wisdom among those interested in tracking movie production costs was that "the bigger they are, the harder they fall." And *Titanic*, at $200 million, was hailed as the most expensive ever. To limit their risk, Twentieth Century Fox and Paramount became partners on the film. As it neared release, special-effects shops across Hollywood worked the night shifts helping Leo DiCaprio's breath appear more pronounced above the cold Atlantic waters, adding strolling passengers to the ship's decks, and deepening the register of the throaty sounds of the propellers' cavitation.

Behind schedule, over budget, and subject to endless speculation over the potential consequences of failure, *Titanic* needed to virtually explode upon the public imagination in order to avoid catastrophe. Thirty-five years ago Fox had produced *Cleopatra*, then the most expensive film ever. And it had nearly sunk the studio.

Fortunately the early buzz about *Titanic* was extremely good. From the pages of *The Hollywood Reporter* and *Daily Variety* to the raves piling up on burgeoning websites, a passionate conversation about the film began to build and build prior to its release on December 19, 1997. Attendees of early screenings were calling the film a three-hankie movie with "must-see" special effects.

Fox and Paramount executives, like their colleagues at other studios, believed in the importance of first-weekend box-office revenues. As films have become bigger and bigger bets, executives now devote greater marketing and promotion budgets to that all-important first weekend. The rules of the game held that one should concentrate spending prior to the opening, "shocking" the system with a flood of messages rather than trying to build awareness gradually. The media had been doing their part to aid the studio: from *National Geographic* specials of the wreck itself to reports on *Entertainment Tonight* on the cast and crew's travails in the Mexican heat (that's why the cold breath had to be added digitally) to business articles pondering the effects of the film on the studio, public awareness was extremely high. By the winter, awareness of *Titanic* was acute for longtime movie buffs, competitors, and casual movie attendees. And the reaction to *Titanic*'s premiere in Tokyo was astonishing, full of sobbing fans and rave reviews.

Other studios were approaching *Titanic*'s potential warily. As "counterprogramming," they aimed their films (like *Flubber* and *Home Alone* 3) at younger audiences. *Scream* 2 had gathered the minds of Gen-Xers, who had created a huge opening, and legs, for the tongue-in-cheek horror film.

When it arrived, *Titanic* produced a hit—the real thing. *Titanic* locked up the screens and locked in the mind-set of millions of moviegoers, and achieved the cultural earthquake equivalent of "The Big One." Theaters routinely turned people away from sold-out shows (effectively expanding the market, and helping competitors such as *Tomorrow Never Dies*, the newest

James Bond film, which enjoyed the highest opening for a Bond film ever).

Titanic had approached and crossed over an *absorption barrier*, meaning that for the moviegoing population a near-permanence had been achieved. It was like the lock-in of Microsoft operating systems in personal computers, except that instead of high technology, this lock-in consisted of ephemeral entertainment. After the show was over, everyone was talking about *Titanic*. Conversations revolved around how exciting the movie was and how it had simultaneously moved people all around the country. *Titanic* had locked in social networks toward a self-sustaining phenomenon that was taking in new fans and converts at a rate greater than the rate at which it would lose steam. The market demand for *Titanic* persisted at the maximum level long after demand for most films had decayed away.

Lock-in for *Titanic* had created a hit on several simultaneous levels: the individual viewer, the small groups of family and friends who came to see the movie together, the audience in the darkened theater, the conversations afterward. Starting with an individual emotional reaction, groups of people had acted as a congealed unit. From tightly packed audiences in separate theaters to disaggregated radio audiences hearing the theme song's airplay, each level of human aggregation had lit up and caused a phase shift in the behavior of the next higher level, until the whole North American society was vibrating to the initial shock of the *Titanic* release. It was as if a crisis had brought people together, like the 1997 ice storms in Maine and Quebec, which left hundreds of thousands without heat in the same winter of the film's release.

And the shock waves were strongest back at the epicenter—Hollywood. Rival executives who released films during that critical month of December had to reassess their strategy, thinking ahead to a time when they could release a blockbuster that could dominate like *Titanic*.

Rules of the Game

Deciding when to release a film is a sophisticated game of chicken among studio executives, as the behemoths mutually decide, through cooperation and competition, when the optimal release date is for a slate of movies. In that sense studios are playing games with each other, games whose rules began to be written a long time ago in the heyday of Hollywood and are still changing today. Understanding how these games work comes from an appreciation of the newly popular game-theory approach to competition.

Many business-school professors and consultants have begun to draw from game-theory to understand how clusters of competing individuals, companies, industries, or even countries form an evolving set of rules as they compete and sometimes cooperate. This is a particularly appropriate way of looking at complex systems, where the simultaneous interactions of players are bound into the emerging rules that are determined by the boundary conditions.

Most game theory taught today, however, is too static. The simple games usually revolve around pricing decisions in market entry—whether a new entrant will command more con-

verted customers with a higher or lower entry price. The outcome depends on what one player thinks the other will do in a
given situation. Each player could think, If I lower prices and
my opponent doesn't, then I'll start stealing customers. As soon
as the other player realizes this, however, he will cut prices to
match mine, maybe even more. Then we'll both be in a spiral-
ing price war that either of us will find it tough to win. In this
simple game, price wars can be avoided, unless one player
thinks he can "get away with it" and leave the other player
powerless to win the lost customers back. Such a game for a
single set of customers that can be won or lost is a zero-sum
game: what's won is lost.

A primer in game theory helps in understanding how
managers can "pay attention to their interactions with competitors, customers, and suppliers, and focus on the end-game, so
that near-term actions promote long-term interest by influencing what these 'players' do," says F. William Barnett of McKin-
sey & Co. in *The Wall Street Journal*. But understanding the games
played in the real world is far more difficult than figuring out
the likely moves in a two-by-two pricing game. In Hollywood,
for example, there are a handful of major studios, each with a
portfolio of films in various stages of readiness for release. The
competitive environment in which a film is released matters a
whole lot. If you have a horror film, would you want to release
it at the same week that buzz is building up for *The Blair Witch
Project*? Game theory and common sense would say that you
would at best end up splitting the pie.

Or how about action? Say you have a nifty idea for a disaster movie about a volcano. Only problem is another studio

not far away has the same idea. This was in fact the case last winter with *Dante's Peak* and *Volcano*, which raced with one another to hit the screens first (conventional wisdom being that the first one out will prevail since moviegoers will perceive the second one as more of the same). Another two-by-two matrix—or actually two and a half, since ABC television aired a made-for-TV movie about volcanoes in that time.

But it really wasn't just a race between these two movies. *Volcano* could have been released by Fox earlier—except that it was also preparing to re-release the *Star Wars* trilogy. These granddaddies of all science fiction films were coming out in a well-publicized re-release just when *Volcano* could take over the race from *Dante's Peak*. So as not to disturb the trilogy, *Volcano* moved back in time, after the release of *Dante's Peak*. And the *Star Wars* re-release? The biggest January box office in motion picture history—until *Titanic* chugged past it.

Strategic Levers

With each picture, motion picture studios have three levers to do battle with their competition: release date, promotion level, and breadth of release in the number of screens showing the movie. All the possible moves and combinations of these levers can give rise to myriad behaviors and outcomes. Add to these levers the portfolio of films that each studio has and the number of studios themselves, and one can find a very rich competitive environment—so rich a set of possible outcomes that almost every encounter is unique. Each time a studio releases a film into a competitive weekend, it faces a situation it has never faced before. There are some things the studio knows, but a lot that it doesn't and won't when the film is released. Moreover, the possible combinations of potential competitive positions is so great that no studio has faced a similar situation before in its history. Each weekend is new, because studios learn what works and what doesn't and build stories about why. The evolution of motion picture competition is filled with perpetual novelty, bounded rationality, and learned behavior, some on point and others mythological and detrimental.

The complexities of the games played in the real world are far more imponderable than the student's two-square payoff matrix. But the simplified model can be instructive, up to a point. The more important set of lessons comes from guiding the rules of the game itself. This is the realm of the metagame, the game about the game being played out. It's a game about setting the rules of the game. That's where *Titanic* played the game brilliantly. The long running time of the film effectively prolonged the time, in weeks, that people could see the film. The film could then enter a position of scarcity (remember the blue Tamagotchis), which worked to provide a buzz for the film, and a position that could lead to a longer "shelf life." And in the sense that first-weekend box-office performance can mean instantaneous success or failure for a film like *Titanic*, getting it right that first time is forever.

Getting hits right may require doing three things right: searching for the hit, building novel intrinsic qualities of the product itself, and nurturing the hit to get it into the hands of the right people at the right time. Add to these three functions something even more important—defining the rules of the game in such a manner that each of these factors can be tipped in the direction of the player who knows best about how the game is played.

But it wasn't just the long running time of the *Titanic* film, or the must-see special effects, beautiful stars, stunning sets, haunting score, or digital breath. It was, in a sense, the coevolutionary combination of all of these factors. They all played on each other to bring out a spectacular whole that transmitted emotional synergy from human to human and led to a predictable audience reaction. But the hit in *Titanic* was even more than that. It was knowing that each of these factors, in concert, played out in the right context, in the proper number of theaters, and given a healthy boost from the fan magazines, television shows, and websites, allowed the game to play into *Titanic's* favor. The game, in this case, was taking moviegoers who would have seen other films and putting them into the seats in front of *Titanic*, week after week. The game was in having the other studios scramble to get out of the way.

Titanic had performed off the charts in our computer model, where we could see our agents waiting to see the film long before it opened. Simulated moviegoers were delaying seeing other films early in December so they could spend their money to see *Titanic* later. And once the film opened, virtually all the computer agents rushed to see it as fast as they could. When shut out, they filled the theaters of their second and third choices. The real game was developing a product that changed the rules of the game just long enough to make the studios a fortune. In this case, the product of *Titanic* included the halo of buzz surrounding it. That word of mouth was unassailable, even if the film came under criticism. The word-of-mouth audience reaction had congealed into a market that had the qualities of persistence, vitality, and perhaps, life itself.

Locking in Lock-In

Such lock-in is not limited to blockbuster films that capture the public's imagination. In the case of *Titanic*, the grip on consumers' conversation and imagination was so rapid and complete that it seemed irrelevant to discuss other entertainment. There are, of course, sustained hits in other industries that also "lock in" mind and market share by tilting their success back on themselves. In practice, this means knowing where social networks exist that will react to your product, realizing how to stimulate those networks to your advantage and your competitors' disadvantage, and sensing when these networks need another jolt of electricity to keep the hit running.

Many hit products solidify their networks by creating new ways to fuel demand, marrying the social conversation with a fluid stream of products. These companies provide myriad opportunities for people to identify with their currency. Consider the Spice Girls, who recorded the number-one-selling CD in 1997 (despite the fact that, as Chris Rock said, "It's impossible to find anyone who bought one.").

The Spice Girls appealed to a tightly knit network of pre-teens entranced by their music, look, and attitude. Among this audience, "Girl Power" (the Spice Girls' handy motto/marketing phrase) reigned, dovetailing with the growth and promotion of women's sports and forthright female characters on television and film. The Spice Girls were more than a smash hit; they were a movement. They sold more than 14 million albums and 20 million singles in under a year, earning more than $50 million. And they did so through more than just snappy pop tunes. Under the savvy promotion of manager Simon Fuller, the group became an international symbol for millions of fans. In fact, a September 22, 1997, *Forbes* article on the group (arguing they had "turned a pop act into a brand name") summed up their appeal quite well:

> Consciously or unconsciously, Fuller is tapping into a cultural phenomenon. The Spice Girls are a textbook case of Daniel J. Boorstin's theory of "Consumption Communities." In his Pulitzer Prize–winning trilogy *The Americans*, Boorstin explained that identity has gone through a subtle but profound shift in the twentieth century. Traditionally people identified themselves in ethnic, religious, or political terms. That's passé. Less frequently do people think of themselves as, say, midwestern Republican Methodists. Now they are less what they believe but more what they consume: "I am a Vouvray-drinking, Mercedes-driving *Vanity Fair* reader."

The Spice Girls locked out competitors with the network effects from their popularity emanating out to their fans. Just as the Monkees had leveraged the stir of their television show, concerts, and albums thirty years ago, the Spice Girls had also spawned an industry tied to their identity. From bomber jackets to calendars, jewelry to magazines and perfume, and even a *Spice World* movie (with tie-in merchandise, of course), the group provided countless opportunities of reinforcing qualities that allowed young fans to display their loyalty to the group. Moreover, the buzz was carried along heavily trafficked websites.

Their hits emerged from the orchestrated release of singles, video airplay, concerts, and promotional appearances around the world—all of which enjoyed an accelerating reinforcement of demand from each other, one that was met by the rollout of products and the burgeoning conversation within the Spice Girls social network. For the initiator who knows all the pieces that require coordination to set the rules in the metagame, it means production of a money machine.

Today most of us in the United States are familiar with the hit known as Martha Stewart, who has masterfully managed the explosion of adulation around her carefully crafted image. The cult of Martha venerates her as a goddess, a cultural beacon, the embodiment of the Kmart shopper's sense of self as homemaker. As a culture maker, Martha Stewart represents an organizing force in people's lives. From the way in which bedsheets coordinate with towels to the handsomeness of one's gardening tools, the harmony of artifacts in a home all serve to shape the environment of that house. Martha Stewart's artifacts present a carefully designed system of potential energy that can be converted into kinetic energy when sparked by individual conversations, fueled by individual shopping experiences, and ultimately catalyzed through the ensuing cultural buzz. This explosion of interest is neither random or accidental. It is guided by Martha Stewart's strong will, acute knowledge of demography, and continual influx of new but related fashion ideas, products, and distribution channels (from magazines to TV shows to websites) that fuel the expansion of the bubble of awareness.

One of the key secrets to Martha Stewart's ability to craft an empire that is estimated to gross more than $200 million annually is her ability to converge her contribution and distribution networks. She has made her network extremely adaptive—by coevolving the passionate interest in her tastes and crafts with an ever-expanding range of products that embody these tastes, which in turn coevolved with the products and the desires of the customers.

Evergreens

Most companies live or die by "evergreens"—perennially valuable brands such as Mickey Mouse or Calvin Klein, images that seem to permanently register a positive response for consumers. But what are evergreens but a virtually permanent lock-in of a brand or image? The Walt Disney Company, for instance, has created a lock-in on a near permanent basis for Mickey Mouse. Initially an animated mouse in one of Disney's first films, Mickey sustained people's interest and identification for decades with attendant reinforcement mechanisms such as clothes, TV shows, and even theme parks.

Titanic appeared in a shock wave at the theaters. And surely over the months and years ahead we will see *Titanic* over and over again as it mutates into rented and purchased videotapes and then transfigures into cable and then broadcast showings. The best example of a film series leveraging its popularity through merchandising is the *Star Wars* episodes. *Episode 1*, a prequel to the original series, introduced new loveable characters, adding billions to the more than $4 billion in box office receipts and sales of toys, books, clothing, collectibles, and the like that the first three films accrued. We can think of *Star Wars* as an evergreen product, much like the Walt Disney Company's Mickey Mouse, delighting children of all ages year in and year out. Each of these toys and plush animals reinforces demand, locks in loyalty, and locks out close imitators.

One of the great toy hits of the past couple of years, based on the popular character Elmo of public television's *Sesame Street*, seems destined to become such an evergreen. "What happened with Tickle Me Elmo happens once a decade in the toy industry—and perhaps even longer," says Neil Friedman, president of Tyco Preschool. Tickle Me Elmo was a cultural earthquake the likes of which hadn't been seen since Generation-Xers went crazy for Cabbage Patch dolls as kids in 1983. As Friedman and executives from Children's Television Workshop, the nonprofit organization that produces *Sesame Street* and handles the licensing of its characters, attest, the success of this giggling plush doll illustrates how smart managers can help lock in and sustain a smash product.

The doll's popularity was so great, and so complete, that the company registered demand for five times the 1.2 million units it sold during the holiday season of 1996. On the day after Thanksgiving, shoppers from coast to coast lined up for hours before toy stores opened to buy the doll. Such a smash constituted a figurative earthquake, one that was subject to the power laws of tremors.

And this hit was an instance of *coevolutionary technology*. All of the components of the toy—the doll's character, his laugh, and even the "tickle" technology—had been around for some time. But the product came to life and enjoyed its shocking success only when independent inventor Ron Dubren brought them together in one product. Suddenly these parts became more than simply their sum total. They hit a phase change in which the parts became radically, fundamentally different than before; and the attendant craze was, not surprisingly, nonlinear.

Finally, Elmo exploded when the white-hot buzz leapt beyond the initial target audience of parents to engage children and teens. Like Beanie Babies, which were sold to kids, yet enjoyed a second wave of popularity when parents began collecting them over the Internet, Elmo rode successive waves of demand in the market. Elmo became more than simply a playful and nonviolent toy for kids; as word of the doll's hipness and scarcity leapt from one trust network to another, the must-have-it status made the doll ever so much more desired. In fact, there was such demand for the doll after it had sold out that scores of rumors about deliberate shortages arose around the country.

Forecasting and Nonlinear Events

Of course, not all products are blockbusters. In fact, fractal laws show that while the massive quakes dominate our hearts and minds, a portfolio of products will include a myriad of small hits and a great number of smaller events. These are subject, nonetheless, to the same laws of nonlinearity as blockbusters. And as such, they demand careful analysis and readiness to adjust one's levers accordingly.

The rate at which a hit takes off is often a function of the demography it inspires rather than the amount or type of marketing message it receives. Word of mouth, which runs faster or slower depending on the age of the consumer, can vary widely in how long it takes to create a hit. *Titanic*, a lesson in shock-wave mechanics (the same model for understanding what happens when bombs—big ones—explode), was loved by people of all ages. But it was the all-important audience of teenagers and young adults who sparked the film's explosion by seeing the movie when it opened—and then viewing it again and again.

Contrast the success of Oscar®-winning *Titanic* with another nominee for Best Picture: *The Full Monty*. Made for $3.5 million by Fox Searchlight, a division of Fox devoted to more avant-garde films, the British-origin film achieved success in a fundamentally different way than *Titanic*. Originally projected to gross perhaps $10 million in Great Britain, the film scored more than four times that amount, becoming the most popular movie ever in that country—until, of course, *Titanic*. As this lively comedy gathered momentum from an older demographic audience, the word of mouth spread at a slow, steady pace—quite different from the shock of *Titanic*.

Economist Art De Vany, who has written remarkable papers about how Hollywood reacts to hits and bombs, posits that the entire industry is built around contingency and adaptivity. It is entirely possible that this flexible model of interconnecting studios, producers, special-effects houses, theater owners, and the like are able to react to the hit, since as De Vany states, "nobody knows what makes a hit or when it will happen. When one starts to roll, everything must be geared to adapt successfully to the opportunities it presents." De Vany's work appears to apply most dramatically when "demand develops dynamically over time as the audience sequentially discovers and reveals its demand." Such a revelation was fully exposed in *The Full Monty*.

According to *Variety*, *The Full Monty* was the most profitable film of 1997, in terms of how well its gross compared to its production costs. Much of this success was due to its ability to catalyze its further success. That is, the story of the movie's success caught the public's attention and whetted moviegoer interest, spurring on ever greater success. Several newspapers picked up the story of the sleeper film that was grossing enormous sums in the United States, Australia, Spain, and France. Executive Lindsay Law, who runs Fox Searchlight, was quoted as saying, "We decided the film was its own best marketing tool." The film's success was due to a slower, steadier, and more measured climb than an explosion like *Titanic*, as older word-of-mouth effects took over like a second stage from the initial marketing booster.

In both cases, and in all launches, executives are looking for evidence of patterns of small bursts of demand in the market; emerging patterns that they can lever to their advantage.

These bursts of demand, as I've mentioned previously, are

called Nonlinear Events, or NLEs. They are the evidence in the market of these early conversations that led to small bands of moviegoers that led to legions of early adopters, and then to vast waves of fans obsessed with talking about a film's virtues. Filmmakers know they are in business of making dreams come true, and Hollywood lore is filled with stories of stars, hits, and bombs. The underlying set of human activities that make these hits and stars are the nonlinear events themselves. The early set of circumstances that, maybe even just by luck, propel a film into the forefront of the consciousness of the minds of many individuals, who make up a vast crowd of similarly motivated people simultaneously around the country, who are motivated, all at once, to negotiate what they want to see with their friends and loved ones, line up, purchase a ticket and some popcorn, and participate in the opening of a market—in the introduction of a new product. And in launching a new idea into the culture.

For an executive whose business may be shaped by the nonlinear events, the questions may be: Do NLEs happen in my business? How can I detect them if they do exist? Do I know what to look for in terms of their shape, persistence, and decay rate? Do they happen on the order of seconds, minutes, months, or decades? How would I know if an NLE was happening—and what does it mean? Most important, how do I respond to NLEs? Once I detect an NLE, what levers can I use to fan the fire—promotion, advertising, free trial to opinion leaders? How can I use word of mouth to my competitive advantage? If I miss this event, will there be others that I can take advantage of—and when I start to recognize their existence, will I get better at seeing them earlier, or in more subtle environments?

Getting good at detecting nonlinear events may be a terrific place to start—by looking for the elements of causation and figuring out how these events may arise, we could take the first few steps to build the systems to more readily detect them earlier in their life cycle. Even more important, in many current business processes, we may have built systems that cause nonlinear events to be erased from our observation tools. The use of averages, steady-state assumptions, noise removal, and trend projection simply erases these critical clues, so it is crucial to be wary of methods that actively remove from product introductions and from our customer's reactions to our actions, the role that NLEs may play in the development of our markets.

TV and TV Game Shows

We have found that managers in hits factories who tap into complexity theory can radically revise how they practice forecasting. Rather than building just three scenarios, which can easily hide the huge hits that occur infrequently yet are nonetheless crucial, they plan for the unplannable.

Conventional forecasting models run through a great many possible outcomes and then build three scenarios: What are the low-, medium-, and high-probability events? Yet this way of thinking is akin to a manager averaging his data. By focusing on the most likely outcome, managers discount low probability events to zero. This does not prepare them for unforeseen outcomes that can have the highest impact. Instead, smart managers understand that preparing for contingencies becomes more important than extrapolating from the present.

Building thousands of futures enables managers to explore different areas of their decision-making space. If you have five strategies, two or three will be dominant, two will be niche-based, and one will be dying all the time. They occupy different parts of the power curve. And the niche-based set of strategic actions may serve as the lifeboat that saves you in the end. Who could have predicted that Westinghouse, which started out in power stations, would today be the owner of one of the largest chain of television stations? This iterative strategy, though it may make sense when considered one step at a time, would never have emerged as a likely scenario under conventional planning.

Moreover, building portfolios enables managers to prepare for low-probability events, and to tap into game theory to augment human thinking that may be either biased, myopic, or emotionally charged. Instead of movies, think of a hit product that must be repeated over and over again to survive—the television show. Television has its own game, played again and again, week after week, year after year: prime-time scheduling.

Since the dawn of the television age, programming schedules have been done by hand, literally, on walls, by moving cardboard rectangles that represent the shows of each network. Now, there is a set of adaptive algorithms that are also placing their digital hands on the schedule, with one simulated network exec trying this and another digitally divined network head answering with that.

Game theory is embedded into the behavior of TV executives reshuffling shows like bridge bids. This process is still done today in exactly the same way as it was since the first nationwide broadcast networks were created. In all, executives search for a match between creativity in shows and the audience they attract. This simple starting premise eventually adapts into complex schemata—such structures as Must-See Thursdays, the counterprogramming of skating against *Monday Night Football*, and other such gamesmanship.

As the simple becomes comes complex over time, advantages are learned, experience by experience. The rewarded structures become reinforced and locked in. When a game is relatively simple, simple strategies emerge immediately as the most effective. But over time, more and more complicated strategies emerge, ever more crafty and useful than the initial strategies that seemed so good at the outset.

At Christmastime in 1997, America felt a strong jolt. Comedian Jerry Seinfeld announced that his show, the mainstay comedy of NBC's Thursday night juggernaut, would end after its current season. Magazine covers heralded the news. Pundits wondered how NBC would be able to retain its stronghold on its well-watched shows anchored by the *Seinfeld* audience. *Seinfeld* wasn't just one of the most popular shows in the television universe at the time; it was also the most valuable by dint of its cherished younger demographics.

NBC, in fact, had pulled itself up from a distant third to the number one spot among networks partly though its domination of Thursday nights. Previously networks had battled for certain critical time spots; NBC had created, through block programming, a strategic beachhead from which it could help fledgling shows take flight. Thursday night essentially belonged to NBC. The game had traversed from simple to complex. And now, this single event had the potential of changing the strategies of the five or six networks, cable channels, premium offerings, and the companies that offered these programs to these distribution outlets.

A few weeks later, another set of programming events occurred. The NFL had received bids on its programming, and the prices offered had gone through the roof. NBC had tried to outbid ABC for their flagship sports program, *Monday Night Football*, but had been unsuccessful. ABC protected this property, and NBC, which was also outbid for its Sunday programming, was left out of football for the first time in thirty-four years. And it didn't stop—NBC then turned around and spent an unprecedented $13 million an episode for the rights to its Thursday night smash *E.R.*

A year before the *Seinfeld* event, we had built an automated television scheduling system that used computer agents as synthetic network executives, digitally moving pieces of cardboard around on a scheduling board in analogy to the actions that real executives take. These game-playing executive agents would look across their schedules, gauging the relative strength of their shows' ratings and popularity against their competitors'. Moreover, the shows themselves tried to rearrange themselves to attract a higher level of audience and boost their ratings. Each show was allowed to move and seek a position against a relatively weak competitor and stay away from other strong shows.

When we first tried these simulations, we found *Monday Night Football* moving to take on the lucrative Thursday night. On other occasions it tried to move to Saturday or Sunday.

When we restricted *Monday Night Football* to Monday night, we found other effects, as most shows stayed away from the dominant NBC Thursday night. The agents discovered the value of winning nights, and other networks tried to take over other nights. The strategies changed in fits and starts; some simulation runs were basically static and boring, while others were marked by prolonged periods of fluid movement to gain temporal advantage. What the simulations accurately predicted was a period of instability in television viewing, one marked by fighting for Thursday night's television audience that had been freed from NBC's grip. Once NBC's stranglehold lessened below a critical level, viewer agents searched for a new attraction. This happened with television programming's hit-seeking evolution, including a return to participitive game shows that directly involved viewers. Engaged, talked-about, must-see spectacles were built for the core of the broadcaster audience, and sparked a network revival, especially for Disney's ABC network.

The wildly popular *Who Wants to Be a Millionaire* show, imported from Europe, where it had proved successful, provided the hit. Once capturing American viewers, *Millionaire's* low-cost production invited other executives to radiate toward other similar programs, including *Greed*.

What the synthetic customers were not able to predict, however, was the turbulence in this new demand wave. Because of the ease of experimenting and extending the original *Millionaire* concept into similar game shows, rapid evolution of new formats, extensions, and failures, such as *Who Wants to Marry a Multi-Millionaire?*, kept the hits' factories churning.

Locking in the Right Buzz

Managers in hit factories operate by a set of principles that are sometimes explicit and sometimes embedded in their behavior. By knowing what levers they have at their disposal (such as the impact of advertising dollars on breadth of opening in the film business), understanding the physics of how patterns evolve in their system, and being aware of what is happening in their world in real time, hit makers can ensure a form of lock-in.

This lock-in operates by the principles of increasing returns—where success begets success, in that a resource becomes increasingly more valuable as more people use it. Yet where the phrase "network externalities" has been applied in the past to such technological networks as phone systems or computer operating systems, the power of social networks is no means less entrenched and dynamic.

This form of emergent behavior means that playing metagames and being able to change the rules of the games is key for managers. Knowing that you are playing games with competitors is important—and taking the iterative steps that tilt the future in your favor is critical. This has significant resonance with the notion of coevolution, which is more than mere serendipity. It is important to know how the factors can work together in a coevolutionary manner, and then like Martha Stewart, or the Spice Girls, help that surprising outcome occur "naturally."

As we have seen, however, lock-in isn't always ideal. When companies find themselves locked into a position that fails to maximize their profits, or sucks the energy out of their system, then these very dynamics work against them. The important aspect here is to determine what broad systemic changes can be addressed to tilt forces in such a way as to build in optimal lock-in. This chapter began to address the questions necessary to identify and sustain lock-in. The next chapter will look at the wired environment in which lock-in occurs, ever more quickly and deeply.

7

HITS IN REAL TIME

Despite any of Al Gore's claims to have gotten the Internet started, the key coalescing event of this fundamentally new societal force took place when a group of disgruntled consumers with otherwise random complaints discovered how the Internet could aggregate their interactions into an entirely new form of discourse.

CEO Andy Grove never thought Intel would take such a beating over the Pentium chip—until it was too late. In the late summer of 1994, a few users had noticed that the company's flagship microprocessor had a minor bug in it. In infinitesimally rare cases, when calculating huge numbers, the chip was accurate only to a certain number of decimal places. In a fax to those few consumers who noticed, the company called the bug a "subtle flaw" and reported that the average spreadsheet user would encounter the problem only once in 27,000 years. Grove, and Intel, were used to such things. Noting the slim risk from this flaw in the part of the chip that does heavy-duty math, Grove rationalized. "This is a long time, much longer than it would take for other types of problems which are always encountered in semiconductors to trip up a chip. So while we created and tested

*ways to correct the defect, we went about our business," he writes
in* Only the Paranoid Survive.

*Intel decided to replace only those chips that it felt deserved
it. This was a classic response from a technology-based company. But something was happening that the company didn't
plan. Over the past few weeks postings had begun to appear on
user groups over the Internet. A letter from Professor Thomas R.
Nicely of Lynchburg College to Intel, detailing the flaw, was
posted by a colleague on a CompuServe bulletin board. Before
long a buzz took over the Internet, reaching such a pitch that a
trade magazine was forced to take note. From there the story
migrated to CNN, and before long, Intel had itself a public-
relations disaster, compounded by the fact that IBM announced
that it would temporarily stop shipments of Pentium-based
computers.*

*When the dust cleared from the Floating Point Unit (FPU)
flap, Intel had corrected the chip design, pulled all their old
materials from production, and replaced chips at customers'
request. Their write-off would total $475 million. And all from
a few buzzing "flames" off the Net.*

In his recent book, Andy Grove writes, "What happened
here? Something big, something different, something unexpected." For Intel, this crisis marked a shift from being a maker
of computer parts to selling a branded product directly to consumers—a strategy that now was rising up against them. They
were operating by an anachronistic paradigm. Intel, interestingly, initially treated the problem like a complicated—but not
complex—one. They took a top-down approach to a bottom-

up problem. As *The New York Times* reported, "Intel officials set to work on the crisis the way they attacked all large problems—like an engineering problem, [Senior Vice President Paul] Otellini recalled. 'It was a classic Intellian approach to solving any big problem,' he said. 'We broke it down into smaller parts, that was comforting.'"

But there was another fundamental change underlying this "hit," as it were—the Internet. The power of the Internet aggregated a few random complaints into a rapid, unified rebellion against Intel. Websites sprang up, collecting and coalescing people's experience with Intel's flawed FPU. Random users who would probably never have had an opportunity to share their common experience could easily find others on user group bulletin boards. Moreover, the furor over the Pentium chip did more than alter the way that Intel handled customer relations. The attention given to, and the ultimate result of, the crusade, showed the public the power of this new medium. The huge impact of the aggregated customer complaints turned out to be, as it were, the "exceptional" that proved the rule. The fact that a group of scattered though like-minded customers of Intel could form an effective voice through the Internet convinced others of the Internet's potential. And as people's belief and interest in the Internet grew, so did their usage. The Internet began to dig its own grooved pathway.

The Intel Pentium flap shows how the Internet not merely revs up the conversation but changes it, shaping what would have been a random bunch of complaints into something much larger—a "hit," as it were. Many of us are familiar with the old Wella Balsam commercial, where one fan of the creme rinse tells two friends about its merits. They in turn each tell two friends, and they tell two friends, and so on, until the television screen is filled with what seem to be thousands of small fans. Such is the nature of meme-propagation on the Web, where stories quickly become fable, and ideas can spontaneously take on the force of a tidal wave. Today a number of prominent Web researchers have commented on the "small-world" nature of websites and Web usage. So-called small-world networks are those in which the individual nodes that are connected are highly clustered, with the distance between any two randomly chosen nodes to be a short one. By comparison, notes researcher Lada Adamic of Xerox PARC, "random groups are not clustered and have short distances, while regular lattices tend to be clustered and have long distances."

The most evocative of small-world networks is what playwright John Guare popularized with the title of his play *Six Degrees of Separation*. This poetic reference alludes to the idea that all people in this world can form a chain of human connection that is comprised of no more than six people. The new friend you meet randomly at a cocktail party, or in an unfamiliar setting, is likely to share a common acquaintance, or certainly know somebody who knows somebody that you also know. This numerical clustering is not limited to human relationships; other networks such as the power grid of the western United States and the neural network of the worm *Caneorhabiditis elegans* also conform.

Moreover, Adamic and others such as researchers Duncan Watts and M. E. J. Newman have noted that the Web itself conforms to the small-world network phenomena. This has particular resonance for the relative popularity of sites; for distributed systems have been shown to display dramatically different behavior within the structural context of small-world networks. Rather than view individual sites as isolated islands where Web surfers visit for a particular reason, people should see them as interconnected hubs of vital information networks. Their success then hinges as much on their role within the network as it does as an isolated hot spot.

Hits on the Internet have a radically faster metabolism than in our carbon world. Word of mouth flies over the Net at a rate unmatched by the chatter at bus stops, the summing up of the day's events over dinner, or even the gossip in schoolyards or slumber parties. Each conversation in the schoolhouse, or any social setting, has its own increasing returns and absorption barrier. Meme passage in a group follows a "lock-in" pattern where a first mover will go out on a limb with an opinion: "I think *Psycho Beach Party* is a cool film," or "I found the wildest website today." This emotional investment—when reinforced by the others—then enjoys the increasing returns of bolstering that person's authority to determine where Web surfers should go, thereby making that individual an even hotter arbiter of taste. On the Web, where unlimited numbers of people can simultaneously participate in a conversation, this phenomenon is cranked up.

On the Web, hits happen in real time. In what has been called a "friction-free" space, seemingly isolated opinions aggregate into movements at an unprecedented rate. Word of mouth that once took place in a chain reaction can take place almost instantaneously; simple computing has given way to massively parallel processing. Individuals form groups without the intervention of third-party hosts; this disintermediation makes the conversation (the force that binds a group together) all the more transparent.

As a result of these qualities, hits on the Web are more prone to the laws of increasing returns than hits in our carbon world. How so? These silicon symbols are simply the hippest ideas made manifest. What makes a website popular? First of all, the fact that it is named "cool" by Yahoo or another Web arbiter of taste catapults it above the random sites. Then, simply by dint of receiving this imprimatur, the site attracts more visitors, which makes it ever more compelling to surfers.

Which websites become hits? Those that are known. Increasing returns certainly accrues to the websites that have drawn a modicum of attention to themselves—which then builds upon itself. Those that have, get. Without a critical mass, sites lose their energy. The threads of conversation dissipate among people, who won't linger on the site because there isn't enough going on there. Living sites, on the other hand, sprout conversation threads constantly.

Consider one of cyberspace's great success stories, the *Motley Fool*. Devised by an irreverent pair of brothers, David and Tom Gardner, the *Motley Fool* was an investment newsletter with no more than a few hundred subscribers that sprang to life when the two posted it on AOL. For the Gardners' site, early success became the currency for it to launch even greater success. As fans developed on the site, they began to converse about "hot" stocks—Iomega, for example, the zip-drive maker, was one of the board's early finds—swapping information directly with one another. The more fans joined in, the more desirable the site became, and, accordingly, the better the reports were. One famous early poster literally visited the company, and through such tactics as observing how many cars were in the lot to handle production demands, reported a coming surge for the company. As the site became "hot," it came to quickly enjoy its own form of "lock-in" for AOL's interested parties.

Eventually, like Martha Stewart, who is brilliant at refunneling the taste and passion of her customers into new products and media, the Gardners grew their website and business, adapting their product constantly into weekly electronic mailings, industry reports, T-shirts and hats, and finally, a string of successful investment books.

As the Web Grows

The Internet itself is a complex adaptive system—one that became a hit with the coevolution of several technological and social factors. As my former fellow Coopers & Lybrand partner Andrew Zimmerman has pointed out:

> The Internet, like most complex social and technological phenomena, represents the coevolution of numerous technologies as well as an emergence of the need, or desire, for their uses. The VCR, another such phenomenon, had been around for decades before it became suitable and desirable for home use. When it achieved that fitness, it caused some fundamental changes in the way people entertained themselves—and it spawned a whole new industry, the video rental business. Similarly, the basic technol-

ogy behind the fax had been around since the 1800s; why didn't it take until the 1970s? Because at that time, a number of conditions coevolved to make the fax desirable. The Japanese embraced the technology because it allowed for faithful, intact transmission of the kanji characters of the Japanese language (very little of which was computer-readable at the time). Prices for the equipment (much of which was manufactured by Japanese companies) dropped, and, in the same period, Federal Express began offering overnight mail delivery, which upped the ante, creating a need for even more rapid delivery of documents. As the technology improved and as the price points fell further, the fax became ubiquitous.

In the 1950s, television exploded onto the scene to become a new phenomenon. Millions of Americans huddled around their sets to watch *I Love Lucy*, which, to borrow a phrase from today, was the "killer application" that inspired millions of Americans to buy a television and thus join the crowd. According to David Halberstam, in April 1952 10.6 million households were watching; by 1954 as many as 50 million people were tuning in. This new medium continued to glue Americans together throughout the McCarthy hearings and the rise of quiz shows.

This new form of media also spawned a new form of public conversation where the method of social interchange goes through a transformation. Though the shows were broadcast by "networks" such as CBS and NBC, the result was a top-down sifting and filtering of information which was then distributed to the nation. People reacted to the nonlinear events of their day through the six o'clock news, which gave shape and meaning to their shared experience.

This new form of conversation was made possible by the rise of a new technology. Lesser forms of social bonding via products also appeared with the coevolution of technology and social change. Consider the spectacular success of Mickey Spillane in the 1950s. He was not just a cultural phenomenon, but a confluence of a set of new technologies. The ability to mass-produce twenty-five-cent books coevolved with his broad popular appeal. This new form of book—cheap, disposable, accessible—may have helped create a market for his type of fiction. Nobody had to justify shelling out big bucks for a somber hardcover tome; instead they could pick up a trifle with their pocket change, and consume it as quickly and easily as a soda.

Today we have the ability to witness—and increasingly participate in—national and international events with an editing mechanism. The rise of the Net has changed the social conversation into more of an interactive and participatory one, binding us more fully to the hits in our lives.

In the 1976 Olympics, a remarkable event occurred. Nadia Comaneci performed a perfect 10 gymnastics routine and earned a gold medal. It was America's bicentennial year, and the country had put together a series of celebrations for the Fourth of July holiday. One celebration didn't happen exactly on time, however. Tens of millions of miles from U.S. soil, the Viking 1 spacecraft was orbiting Mars. A landing site had not been chosen, and the Martian terrain seemed unexpectedly rough and hazardous. Scientists and engineers nervously looked over hundreds of square miles of Martian plains, hoping to find a smooth spot that would be safe to land on, yet likely to hold a soil that could contain evidence of biological life. The planned landing date, July 4, came and went, and the big announcement that an American spacecraft had landed on the surface of Mars never happened. Reporters grew tired of waiting during the two weeks it took for the landing to occur. Sometimes outside events can intervene and completely destroy the emerging hits process—knocking a growing dynamic to pieces.

When it finally came, the landing was successful and inspiring to those who cared. But time had run out, as it were; *Time* magazine ran Nadia Comaneci on the cover, while the Martian surface garnered a corner insert. People's attention had already shifted to the next big thing. The space program moved on to the shuttle era, and the public got used to seeing people in orbit around the earth.

A little more than twenty years later, an intrepid band of scientists and engineers at CalTech's Jet Propulsion Lab, the same lab where I had been a part of the Viking flight team, successfully landed a small spacecraft called Pathfinder on the surface of Mars. This time, though, the public reaction was altogether different. Pathfinder had a website that showed images from the surface of the planet almost as soon as they were received here on Earth. Pathfinder had a small rover named Sojourner, and the scientists took to naming the rocks around the spacecraft that the rover visited. The website became a phenomenon, and was soon one of the most visited sites on the Internet.

This website was one of the most popular in the short history of the Internet, breaking records of visits as the curious continued to pore over these fascinating pictures of another world. The immediacy and accessibility of the technology helped make the Pathfinder experience so personal for millions of people. The simultaneity of the experience, along with the fun of looking at these rocks that had familiar-sounding names, brought the Martian experience home to a nation that could virtually explore the planet themselves. This helped spark the trigger of human interest in a little remote-controlled rover, and the wave of a word-of-mouth hit that spread from the computer linkages into the website. This interest was sustained, in fact, through the two failed missions that followed the Pathfinder mission. Like sequels to blockbuster movies, these expeditions expanded the story to the community of the curious who were originally nurtured through the first trip, and the accompanying story.

Shopping on the Web has a fundamentally different nature from shopping in our carbon-based environment. On the Web, consumers attach themselves to the products at a deeper and more personal level than at a record or book store, largely as a result of participating in a real-time, ongoing conversation among like-minded people conducted through the products. The best websites help form and amplify the community that people form with other buyers around a specific purchase.

Consider the rise of Amazon.com, which not coincidentally has enjoyed a "winner-take-all" share of the market for consumer purchasing on the Web. The company itself has leveraged its early establishment of an identity as the cyberspot to buy books into a burgeoning strength as the most successful

Web company to date. Sprinting to the motto of "Get Big Fast," Amazon.com set its own grooved pathways of success through designing a satisfying and reliable customer experience on the site. During the first few years of the company's hyper-growth, the growing reputation of the site became a key attractor for new cyberbuyers; the company also shrewdly used its rapid stock growth as a form of collateral for raising more than $1 billion in convertible bonds.

The company wisely leverages the scope and intensity of its customer's experiences as one of the key offerings to the community. Curious as to a good book to buy? Then you can choose from one of many customized suggestions. First of all, you can check the running, constantly updated list of Amazon's bestsellers in a myriad of categories for a sense of what is popular. You can browse another form of bestseller list: Amazon's famous "purchasing circles," which break down popular books by company, region, and other customer affiliation.

Or, you can go to the pages of books you have enjoyed and read the comments and critiques of other customers. You can participate in this ongoing conversation yourself through posting reviews of your own. Or you can look to the bottom of the page to see what people who bought books that you like also purchased. Or, after buying several items yourself, you can enjoy the personalized recommendations that Amazon.com makes for you based on their own computer programs, which are themselves determined by the aggregated behavior of their own customers.

The cybershopper on this constantly changing information environment is not merely satisfying an impulsive urge to buy an item (though certainly the site is set up for that). The individual becomes part of an ongoing conversation; shopping becomes a form of collective entertainment.

Consider eBay, another Gorilla site of the Internet. Passionate hobbyists with an opportunity to trade collectibles such as Pez dispensers or Pokémon cards have built this site into one of the most heavily visited Internet areas, and have catapulted the company to a more than $8 billion market capitalization. eBay has done more than simply allow nostalgic collectors to find long-lost treasures. eBay has turned the art of the auction, the hunt for personal passion objects, into a shared quest. Many individuals who trade on eBay have become far more committed to the social networks they have formed on the site than to any particular artifact they have purchased. Shopping has become the vehicle for people to connect with one another.

Making Sense of Web Hits

One of the most important qualities of the Web is the fact that it conducts transactions and conversations and collects data in near-real time. The result is a blizzard of data in mouse clicks, page requests, and software downloads. To make sense of this, managers can learn from living systems. Dealing in near-real time is how we have learned to deal with the complexity and the nonlinearities of the real world. You don't see human beings with spreadsheet devices that smooth out bumps and flatten spikes; rather, you see people with eyes and ears; you see consciousness. The challenge of utilizing the Web is in linking back to what living systems do.

How would a living system make sense of all this data? By

sensing, storing, and remembering it, and by finding the significant patterns in all this activity. In this environment, that means having a radar for the affective states that give a clue as to when something important is happening. It may simply be that a group of people—as represented by their proxies on the Web—are all visiting the same site, or simultaneously purchasing similar products at an electronic store. The fact that so many of them are at the same place at the same time may indicate that they are happy to be there. The key to making sense of patterns on the Net is understanding how to infer the affective states of agents, because emotions are what coalesce the bonds that are taking place where there is a nascent hit. Trying to understand the affective state of agents—just like a living system would—is key to seeing hits emerge.

These managerial tools help people understand what is happening. They enable them to see the people transiting to the website and get a sense of whether they are satisfied with their experience there by painting a picture. These pattern-recognition programs look at the transit history of each agent—or human being—as he or she goes through a website, and try to classify them on the basis of their behavior. It asks what can be inferred about an individual's behavior. Based on their history of taste and behavior, we can make a judgment, an inferential guess about their future actions.

What happens with data? When managers or analysts examine detailed company information, they often try to make sense by averaging, summing up, and taking only infrequent snapshots of the way their business is run—all of which eventually blindsides executive management to any minor perturbations and fluctuations in these operating numbers. Aggregating the numbers destroys every sort of nuance or sign of problems at the most detailed level.

Understanding this urgency for detail lies at the heart of making sense of electronic commerce. Playing down these fluctuations from electronic commerce would once again do nothing more than destroy information. There is another way: retaining this data as a sense of running the company in near-real time—just as we run our own bodies. Information flows through us. Some is retained, some is thrown away; the most important is remembered. We remain true to the enormous fidelity of the currency of the world that we live in.

Likewise, cybersites must generate and present real-time data in a sensible manner. Say we are looking at a bookseller on the Web. What management needs is the electronic equivalent of looking over the railing and seeing where people are browsing and what they are buying. It would be almost like watching the stock exchange, complete with screaming traders in bright jackets and the roar of activity on the floor. People need a *feeling* for what is happening on this website, one that is, however, drawn from what is actually going on. They need to be able to find what I called in chapter 4 the "ground truth."

The Buzz Is the Hit

Previously in this book we have talked about how word of mouth sells products, and how, in fact, that buzz becomes essentially bound into hits. With the interactive, dynamic, self-organizing quality of the Web, we can now see this principle at the logical extreme: where the buzz around hits—and potential hits—literally *is* the product.

Such is the case with Hollywood Stock Exchange (HSX), a two-year-old website launched by Max Keiser and Michael Burns, a pair of former Wall Street traders. HSX has devised a market where people can register for free at the site and receive $2 million Hollywood Dollars (the virtual currency of HSX), which is held in a money-market type account that draws interest. Users can then invest this scrip in securities that are priced according to the anticipated performance of movies and Hollywood stars, called MovieStocks and StarBonds. Security prices fluctuate based on supply and demand in the market. HSX enables users to trade shares of a MovieStock through its various stages of maturity: concept, development, production, and release. Four weeks after the film's release, the security is delisted at a price that reflects the actual box-office performance. Thus traders jockey to predict the four-week box-office take of each film.

HSX is a great example of a self-organizing system, a conduit for buzz. Interestingly, the popularity and growing sophistication of the site has helped it become a true leading indicator for how films may do. As it has begun to better reflect popular taste, the site has been catching the attention of studios, which are now reported to be thinking of floating potential movie ideas over HSX, and then using the market's reaction as an indicator of whether to proceed or not. In essence, this synthetic market could improve its own predictive value through converging on the real world it tracks.

HSX points out the way that agents on the Web can ultimately track back to our carbon world. Here's what Net pundit

Esther Dyson has written about HSX in her newsletter *Release 1.0* (September 22, 1997):

> HSX is a Trojan Horse. In the course of creating HSX, Burns and Keiser noted the increasing importance of fiat currencies such as frequent-flyer miles, credit-card purchases rewards, and other affinity systems. They predicted that cyberspace would be filled with such systems—say Calvin Klein bucks, Starbucks, Saturn Scrip, and so on—and that these pseudo-currencies would at some point become exchangeable and perhaps even convertible to real currency. But how would that happen? What would act as a U.S. dollar-like reserve currency?
>
> They reasoned that a visible online currency would have to be pegged to a credible, collaterizable core value system, which would give the currency what Keiser calls "plausible accountability." Keiser explains, "The world's economies are based on stuff—physical assets. As the non–Internet economy moves from atoms to bits, virtual currencies will become more of a factor. Someone has to create it. The dollar is based on faith. On the Net, [currencies] should be based on intangibles, like maybe time or ideas. So why not a virtual currency based on ideas and memes."

As an adaptive system that changes according to the participatory nature of the people on it, the Internet has become the place where ideas and passion become the currency of hits for both managers and consumers. The Internet magnifies buzz and pushes the interactive dynamic of buzz to a logical extreme. Given its popularity and immediacy, there are new strategic levers being built to make managerial sense, to sense Web hits and to change rules of social connection and conversation without competitive notice. What's at stake is the shape of the world to come—the Internet world and the real world. Web-based hits that are shaped and levered now can guide the pathways for our collective future, just as today's world is built on the echoes of the hits of our collective past.

8

HOW HITS PERSIST

It takes a leap of faith to get things done.

—Bruce Springsteen

Along the beachfront of Cranston, Rhode Island, sits a string of luxury condos with a beautiful view of the waves rolling off Narragansett Bay. Built during the spasm of excitement of the late eighties real estate boom, these properties embody the wild optimism of the time whence they came. Their elegant New England–style architecture includes full picture windows that reveal views out to courtyards with flowers and a small, attractive harbor in which float sailboats and yachts. And yet these pricey properties came to serve as a deeper symbol of the dangers of booms: lying unoccupied for years, leaving behind a string of bankrupt developers and failed banks.

Today the homes are occupied. In the early nineties, they slowly, gradually began to sell. Purchased for far less than the lowest dreams of the developers who hoped to profit from them, they are nonetheless occupied, and a neighborhood now perches up to the ocean. Though the boom burst, the homes remain, and within them a new community is emerging.

Long after hits have subsided, long after the waves break and the bubbles burst, we continue to reside within the changes they leave behind. These temporary explosions leave a legacy of near-permanent change, and that is the landscape, both literal and physical, that we occupy.

There are artifacts in this world that persist after the hit, which shape our lives. And so while hits seem to rise like stars and eventually fade out, most actually do persist in a different form. The song hits of yesterday become today's classic rock. "Oldies" become standard movie programming, airing continually on cable television. Bell-bottom pants and disco music eventually rebloom, sometimes as a kitsch statement that reframes current tastes and sometimes as simple nostalgia. Take a film such as the recent comedy *Austin Powers*: it reassimilated and reinvented a range of past hits from the late sixties, among them mod fashion styles and the camp allure of James Bond films. Renewing these so-called fads gives them new staying power.

Whether you love or hate the Spice Girls, it's hard to deny that they persist. And while it's hard to say where they'll be in a year, you can bet you'll still be hearing songs like "Wannabe" on the radio in the new millennium. The unprecedented success of *Titanic* will likely change the way Hollywood executives think about blockbuster films. Change agents, who are usually talked about in the context of companies, come and go; but the changes they effect can linger long in the company's history.

Automobile stylings persist after hits, and even such basic foundations as cities and homes are (nearly) permanently altered by the waves of change caused by popular movements. Cultural and technological hubs such as Silicon Valley or Hollywood have become the centers of their industries through first-mover advantage. Once a few critical decisions were made to locate companies or talent in that geographic location, the site locked in its buzz, its qualities, and therefore became ever more populated because of its very success. Such centers enjoy increasing returns of location, and continue to do so even after the metabolism slows down.

These changes seem to come out of nowhere, and have a lasting impact. In *The Beak of the Finch*, author Jonathan Weiner speaks of the evolution of the finches in the Galápagos Islands. He says that true evolution occurs when there is an actual stress in the environment, one that that steers the entire population to another threshold—*which may not be optimum*. And this form of natural selection is not a gradual drift towards changes and mutations, but a sudden rush of change. A recent *New York Times* article posits that global warming, for example, may seem like a slow, gradual process; but a recent article posits that it could occur explosively. That is, though it appears that the earth is warming by a degree a century, that process begets a lake building up on the bottom of Antarctica, which causes the entire ice shape to surge, and lo and behold, the entire ocean moves up a foot or two within six or seven weeks. What appears to be a slow and steady change produces a nonlinear hit; and then the system settles back, persisting as something different.

The Dark Side of Hits

This lock-in of suboptimal conditions could be called the dark side of hits, and applies to such critical processes as the role of real estate in general and of commercial real estate in particular in the creation of wealth in a geographic area.

In the first chapter we looked at the bank collapse in Rhode Island, which went through a robust boom and then a sudden and horrifying bust situation. Yet what few people saw, or acted upon during the boom period, was a pattern of self-reinforcing speculation with no corresponding basis in the real world.

The optimism of the boom, the sense of endless profit for developers who could borrow construction money on increasingly shaky ground, led to many ill-adapted (to use the biological metaphor) condos and other properties. Today they've been absorbed and repurposed, and in retrospect are seen as valuable property. The character of locations such as Cranston has been changed for our lifetime as a result of this boom and bust.

Charles Tansey, a former commercial banker from New York, helped set up and initially manage the agency that liquidated the closed RISDIC institutions and paid out depositors. He believes that the principles of complexity clearly underlie the boom and the bust. He also believes that the principles of complexity can be used to build an early-warning system that would moderate the swings in the real estate lending business and reduce the magnitude of the inevitable losses.

The Rhode Island story shows that whole systems can develop and lock in patterns that become untethered, a web that is tied only to itself.

Here's how Tansey describes the situation:

The most striking thing about this was *not* the fraud, campaign contributions, or corruption. Those are symptoms, not causes; and as the S&L crisis amply demonstrated, these symptoms are by no means confined to Rhode Island. The most striking thing about this crisis was its sheer normalcy—its parallels to so many other booms and busts in the lending business. The Oil Patch, the Third World, Highly Leveraged Transactions—these are all situations over the past two decades where lending discipline is sacrificed for what appears to be a win-win situation, where too much money ends up chasing too few assets, and tens of billions are thrown down the drain.

What's fascinating about the RISDIC crisis is that the legislature had good reason to allow credit unions to do what the credit unions wanted: make speculative real estate loans; carry deposit insurance of up to $750,000, and suffer minimal regulatory intervention. Real estate development was good for the state economy. The well-meaning legislator saw construction jobs, rental income, legal fees, interest income, furniture sales, a higher property tax base— all good things. And where was the risk? Well, from a simplistic standpoint, as long as more loans were coming into the system, pushing up real estate values, the traditional appraisal tools for evaluating risk actually showed the risk to be *decreasing!* So who is the accountant or state regulator to say "slow down!"?

Looking back on the economic bust of Rhode Island, one can see how it conformed to many of the emergent qualities that identify hits as we have defined them. How could a robust and expanding local economy mutate into a fiscal wasteland overnight? In Rhode Island, as Tansey points out, the various parties—the legislators, the bankers, the developers, and the homeowners—all worked together in a way that changed the way they operated.

There were elaborate and varied trust networks that locked in both prosperity and peril. But they were subject to a "lunatic fringe" at the margins of distributions that made for risky loans and brought down the whole system.

Because bankers were making loans based on what the market was saying properties could be worth, as opposed to a more intrinsic quantifiable value, these loans were completely dependent on the collective mind-set, the current conversation about value and prosperity. Appraisals shifted as the collective mind-set shifted. When appraisals were based on the comparable values of other properties in the market, this locked in a pattern where people's hope for a continued boom helped make it so. When collateralized loans are doing well, that's fine. Everything works and grows in an orderly manner. But when they go bad, then they go south in an asymmetrical crash.

What can be done to avoid such collapses? Leaders hoping to effect broad systemic change must search for clues that signify a danger point. Tansey believes that changing the language of lending represents a high-leverage action that could ultimately smooth out the boom-and-bust cycle and direct the system toward a more productive coevolution. In the case of real-estate-backed lending, Tansey believes that basing loans on solid cash flow projects rather than simply basing them on the going agreed-upon comparable value would help tether the bubble back to reality.

Rhode Island is a microcosm of the dangers of ingrained policies that don't react to the changed world in an adaptive manner. They are appropriate to a world that is in the past. We tend to hold on to all our belief systems about how things work even in the presence of hard empirical evidence that things change. Such mental lock-ins become reinforced by societal frames. People have a lot of reasons to not want to change these regulations. Thus they allow these conditions to move closer and closer to criticality. The whole system moves as close to chaos as it can, approaching a gaseous chaotic state where the only question about collapse is when it will happen. Who will pull their money out first and cause the system to collapse?

Here we see the dangers of group thinking, and the promise of policies that can spot when systems seem to be at the breaking point. By spotting when a system might be on the verge of going critical, a public official or planner might be able to have some impact on such important issues. What if you had software that would tell you if there were dangerous patterns developing—that might alert you when the system was nearing a plunge, or that could tell you when other significant patterns were forming in other systems? One potential way to avoid the dark side of hits is to use simulations to forecast when large systems might be headed for danger.

Future History

Drive through Vermont, and you will see remnants of a two-hundred-year-old landscape, much is as it was when the first virgin forest was taken down. Drive quickly, and you see only the newly built condos near the ski trails. Drive slower and you can detour to mountaintop farms, and towns that started growing, but never got the spark of life that allowed them to flourish and prosper. The town of Braintree has a town square at the top of a hill not far from where the industrial mills and town center are today. But the town square remains, an artifact of town planning that lost its purpose. Nearby, other towns have developed their tourist facilities, or have encouraged ski areas to prosper; outlet centers have brought necessary revenue from passersby.

Why did some towns evolve in one direction or in another? And why did some towns get swallowed into cities while others became fossilized? Could townspeople see it coming, and is this the outcome they desired, or did it just happen? And what about the future: Could a planning system help townspeople to gauge the measure and direction of their evolution and steer it in another direction?

Treewell is a computer-based simulation that is a microcosm of a real Vermont town. Although certainly not everything about a Vermont town is represented in the program, many of the essential elements are. Simulated in the program are people who live, work, and shop in Treewell, buildings in which these activities take place, land upon which these buildings exist, and land-use issues upon which the residents of Treewell can vote. Treewell serves as a prototype for the direction that land-use, demographic, and transportation forecasting may point. Agents (which represent individual household heads) that inhabit and visit Treewell can buy and sell land, work in town, shop at the various stores, decide to build or demolish structures, buy land or buildings for farmland or historic preservation, and vote on local land-use issues proposed by their town council. Time will pass in Treewell and users will be able to see the land-use and economic changes that occur.

Hits and Bits

Can we really build a machine to model human behavior, and use that machine to predict the growth of hits in a number of business settings? Perhaps for now the best we can do is to build a machine that can do better than the machines in place today. To make this forecasting machine we must go beyond our old linear model. In that regard, practitioners don't actually need the machine to gain insights into how this new perspective could be useful in guiding their business. It is a good start that this model embraces the chaotic and unpredictable nature of hits rather than shying away from this difficult-to-handle quality.

But there's the promise of more, of learning from and profiting by our hits. We can get close enough to forecast these important events in human cultural history, and therefore be useful. To build this machine, we must use our available technology and throttle back our goals in terms of forecasting precision and foresight to meet the capabilities we can provide. We can strive for what Murray Gell-Mann describes as "that dim searchlight to tell us where the cliffs are, and aren't." And we try to do better with our forecasting machine than the numerical techniques and heuristic approaches that are in place today. We don't need to model conscious human behavior to give a forecast that is "good enough"; we don't need to model humans with all their cognitive capabilities to build a practical model of the behavior that humans exhibit when they encounter hits. In fact, we do pretty well in forecasting hits when we model humans as detached beings who come together in groups around their "passion" over certain ideas and products.

It's hard to imagine that little pieces of code that send messages to each other, that have primitive emotions and that worry about whether they're popular can end up producing a predictive tool. And yet these silicon beings give us valuable insight into our carbon world. We can now see that the same hit-making synthetic mechanism that begat the emergence of grunge music can be transformed, on a different scale and frequency, to apply to other completely different industries. And with the use of game theory, we can extend the notion of single hits to the waxing and waning of fortunes in the technology, manufacturing, and entertainment industries.

There has been a lot of ground in between musical hits and industrial dynamics. The Spice Girls and *Titanic* are really faddish hits. But those agglomerations of behavior that produce frenzies associated with fads around the Spice Girls and *Titanic* don't appear to have a profound impact on the world. Liking or disliking the Spice Girls will not cause empires to crumble or destabilize currencies. And yet, armed with an understanding of how these situations arise and persist, we can better position ourselves to take action if things go wrong. When we have a hit, things can go wrong in an asymmetric fashion—big, bad, and fast. This power law applies to us in myriad effects: some of us have lost our jobs, homes, and systems of government to the same mechanisms of hit phenomena. Little pieces of emotional, talkative, and popularity-seeking code can tell us about hits in music—and in such areas as bank runs, urban development, and political movements. Perhaps they could help us to understand when these forms of situation could be perilous.

Policy is written by humans, and often revolves around a set of guidelines, rules to invoke in given situations. And we know that those rules can get byzantine and baroque as more and more features and conditions are added. These policies can become complex, in order to handle the complex situations where they are supposed to guide behavior, but they are typically a set of fixed rules. Look at the tax code, customs rules for international trading, Medicare rules, and banking regulations, to give a few examples that have intricacies that are at or beyond the limit of human understanding. But maybe not beyond the capacity of software that is adaptive. And maybe that software could even tell where the next likely set of rule changes could appear, because the external dynamics of the world have caused an immediate obsolescence of the rules that are in place. Policy-making simulations have started with human role playing. These simulations are the stuff of business schools and executive training. Now we can inject human emotion into the players. Moreover, public policy may now concentrate on nurturing and listening to individuals in the world rather than categorizing voters and citizens into aggregate blocs.

But there now may be a time for a model that goes beyond the mechanical to a version of a tool on every desktop that can adapt to new information, sense the buzz from a group of software-based observers and talkers, all with divergent perspectives. These perspective-producing situation analysts could help a manager tell when something isn't quite right.

And it could help that manager start to ask what-if questions about the consequences of pulling certain levers as a result of picking up this emerging pattern. In that sense, it can help him tilt the future toward what he wants, by doing the right thing at just the right time.

Hits Are Us

Hits represent an organizing force in our near-chaotic world. As human beings, we collect experiences. We accrete them in our brains, which is how we learn. Leading thinkers such as Danny Hillis, Chris Langton, and Marvin Minsky believe that we are entering a new state of combined consciousness, one in which the Internet reinforces our behavior, leading us to act in a simultaneous manner, as a single organism. It is always extremely difficult for us to see that we are part of something larger, but in fact, if we look at fads and our role in making those fads happen, we are indeed conduits for meme-passing. When Internet users and all those touched by them live in an ever more connected way, we become part of the neural fabric at a human level of getting hits going and making them persist. From an aggregate level, when you gauge the public reaction to hits such as *Titanic* or news events like the death of Princess Diana, it looks as though a single unit were acting, as if this happening were either planned from above—or was a mere coincidence. In fact, while these waves may appear to be random, our participation in these hits, and with each other, may be gauged, perhaps, by the degree of connectedness we are able to achieve through the Internet, combined with personal conversations and broadcast media.

Roger Penrose, the preeminent mathematician and author of *Shadows of the Mind*, has struggled with the feasibility of understanding consciousness through the use of computers and science. He believes that existing methods of computation and science will not allow us to explain consciousness and human intelligence. While I agree that we have fundamental barriers to cross to understand the depths of human consciousness, we may have made a small, halting step toward developing a useful set of human methodologies that we can use to better understand collective behavior.

Will our little adaptive pieces of software ever become part of a conscious-generating machine? Not likely. But that is not what we have set out to accomplish. The notion merely gives us pause that this forecasting machine can ever be truly complete. We are unlikely to generate humanlike thought in any machine that truly mimics the actions of real human beings in generating hits. But maybe we don't need all that computational power, much less consciousness, to help make sense out of hits as they happen. Just a crude early-warning system can be useful. If we can understand how nonlinear events happen, we may be more sensitive to seeing them around us. The incomputability of human conscious behavior can remain forever apart from our feeble beginnings in building the prototypical minds in our software agents.

In our work at PricewaterhouseCoopers, which is deeply informed by those who have plowed the field in complexity research, we are trying to establish a new way of looking at how the world appears to work, a way that has been obscured by our own historical and acceptable methods of thinking and the tools we use to make sense of our world as we know it. What we've done isn't Galileo's telescope, and no, it doesn't shift us from the center of the universe. Yet it may help us better understand how things happen all around us. No doubt it is significant that we get somewhat realistic crowdlike behavior from the interactions of thousands of socially aware bee brains. They aren't truly aware of the real world; they respond to just the limited set of sensory signals we strip out of the world and send to them. And no, they really aren't bees, they are much dumber, as they couldn't tell a real flower from plastic, much less dance the hive dance. But their behavior is nonetheless instructive.

We agree that there are large portions of phenomena in the universe that we have no clue how to simulate, and that the universe clearly includes the consciousness of humans; Penrose even states that there are some models, "with clear-cut rules of evolution, that are impossible to simulate." And even more crushing, Penrose states the powerful case of the mathematician Gödel, whose results "established that human understanding and insight cannot be reduced to any set of computational rules." Penrose uses Gödel's argument to assert that "there must be more to human thinking that can ever be achieved by a computer, in the sense that we understand the term 'computer' today." Nevertheless, Penrose admits the possibility of useful computational systems based on chaotic systems that have "elaborate and effectively unpredictable behavior," that could contain "the key for effectively modeling the effectively non-computable behavior of the mind. For such a thing to be the case, it would be necessary for these chaotic systems to be able to approximate non-computable behavior—an interesting possibility in itself."

Penrose then makes the case, substantiated by elaborate proofs, that while modeling these chaotic systems could help in understanding consciousness, the possibility of actually building such systems is remote at best. He also believes we will fall into an abyss we will not be able to escape with the mathematical tools that we have today. That is where the role of emotions comes in. Emotions link us to affective computing and allow us to mimic the behavior of real humans with very primitive pieces of software code. While we may not have created beings that literally feel sad and happy, their motivations and behavior mimic their breathing counterparts in the carbon world. From these synthetic people we naturally see that people who are correct early on become fashion leaders and risk takers and innovators. And that large portions of the population will stand behind these shocking people, watching what they do, and seeing if there is a sense from the group that what they are doing is an acceptable practice. When enough followers agree that this new behavior is acceptable and do it themselves, then the whole system lifts off and moves from one place to another.

From I-It to I-Hit

Ultimately, it is the role of emotions that makes all these principles relevant to the world we live in. To make the ideas I've talked about in this book work you have to believe in them. It's that simple. By simply believing in your hits you can help make them so.

In essence, there is no observer and observed in the complex world, which operates by the rules of quantum, not Newtonian, physics. One of the key tenets that stands in the gulf is Heisenberg's uncertainty principle, which holds, essentially, that any experiment is changed by the observer. Understanding how hits happen demands a passion for possibilities—the willingness to see patterns that may be sparked by your very own passion to learn.

In the genesis of complex adaptive systems, nonlinear events start with individuals, and build into explosions one transaction at a time. This is no time for detachment. Imbuing ground zero with your own heat and heart helps create the future you desire, no matter how remote the possibility may seem. Nobody can say exactly when a system is poised for a phase change; but we can say with certainty that it takes but the smallest factor—Per Bak's next grain of sand will be the one to cause the landslide. How do we know beforehand that the next one will be the one? They are all minute and carry the same momentum as they cascade down the hill. Instead, look to the passion of one person to represent that single grain of sand. The will is enough to start a fad, convert a random collection of opinions into a cohesive bloc, and launch an idea—or meme—on a journey by which it will replicate countlessly, creating a vast and different result from a simple starting block.

Conversations display increasing returns. Early movers who launch conversations can attain a status of lock-in through those conversations, even when positing an ill-formed, even random idea. Early statements in conversations can lead others who later join in to interject points that amplify or extend those early points of view, even though they were perhaps misinformed or naive. In a business-school class, I once opened a business case and became a champion of a viewpoint about how to solve the case through an organizational change. I immediately gained a following through my initial statements of logic and referential knowledge. But slowly the professor introduced other perspectives. My first-mover advantage, once so strong and convincing to students around me, was waning, to the point where I alone was standing on the branch that was being sawed away from the main trunk. I had lasted a good long time, and gained many followers in my enthusiastic efforts, but those converts were now lured away by dint of the evidence brought to light that argued against me. I almost locked the class into a suboptimal solution. How many other business managers have also locked into early solutions that later seemed inappropriate, and through the fear of embarrassment have resisted change, even in the face of persuasive reasons to make the move to a new direction?

Injecting your own spirit, or passion, into the system helps you form your own grooved pathways. Martin Buber, one of the great philosophers of the twentieth century, posited that mankind exists in two states: I-It and I-Thou. We can have an objective, detached connection with another person as "it," seeing them only in their roles and connection to us through rank or circumstances. When we attach closer bonding, we can achieve the "thou" level of connection. And these connections can somehow crystallize into a larger, holistic structure, melting away the more detached "it" bonds and replacing them with tighter "thou" bonds. Complex adaptive systems have this enveloping property, one that encompasses each individual into a larger, emergent whole.

The fad of the Spice Girls, for example, is the product surrounded by an aura of hysterical fans. The fans wouldn't be hysterical without one another, or without the catalyzing hit product itself. There is a trust network that is built up, of belief in the opinions of others, of the validity of the memes or information and argument that transit from one person to another in this connected web. And the web ultimately encompasses more that the individual nodes along this trust network among friends and fad-mates.

Participating in complex adaptive systems through believing in them holds the potential to transcend this initial set of loosely attached "I-It" links, to somehow connect the I and the Thou. Direct involvement forms a structure that itself orders the chaos around us simply through the act of belief in each other along that trust network. Many a philosopher has spent time defining faith, or belief, but in the context of networks, and communities, I rely on Buber's proclamation that "all living is meeting."

Sometimes when consulting with clients the phrase "leap of faith" comes up. I must be very careful about how I use the phrase, which sometimes is meant to connote a blind jump from one position to another simply to justify a statement that cannot otherwise be proven. But the set of decisions that have produced a point in the business landscape where one firm has found a satisfactory business may not be good enough as the dynamics change. We may need a nudge, a new set of perspectives and a convincing argument that our business is out on that limb, ready to be sawed off. To move off that comfortable position is often scary, especially when people put on a suit of armor labeled *risk management* that reinforces the lock-in of the comfortable status quo. To move from that comfortable position to another unfamiliar and maybe more optimal point involves this leap of faith. And it will be difficult enough, if not impossible, to move with the degree of detachment that characterizes the "I-It" bond. To make the move also means using faith, belief, and passion to form the final link in what is otherwise a complete chain—where the mere act of believing completes a pattern that is now palpable, alive, and meaningful. In this ephemeral and ethereal world of hits, that kernel of faith becomes a real thing that connects one to another—that is, the idea of a product, the product itself, and the passion around that product are all wrapped up together.

Making Sense of New Worlds

Twenty years ago, I told my friend Charles Tansey about my thoughts on the origin of intelligent life. At the time, I was among the first to gaze upon and study images of the surface of a new world—Mars. I looked for patterns on that unfamiliar planet surface with human eyes, eyes that were used to patterns that were more close to home. As part of a team of explorers, we were looking for evidence of life on another planet of our own solar system.

And to gather this intelligence we sent robotic spacecraft far into the heavens. We hoped to imbue intelligence into these early explorers. I explained to Charles my thoughts about patterns and randomness, and how intelligence could possibly arise by mimicking the behavior of some of the most primitive life on this planet, the trilobites. This animal was the earth's biologic equivalent of generations of hit makers in rock and roll music—ubiquitous, persistent, and capable of incredible variations of form on the original design. Perhaps by trying to understand how trilobites learned, we could understand how to build learning spacecraft that would, in turn, learn about patterns in the new worlds they would encounter.

This book represents a step along a journey toward understanding and fulfilling a quest to make sense out of our nonlinear world. In this case, it's the world of consumer demand in business. It's a long way from discovering patterns of ancient arroyos that once carried rushing floods of water into a Martian ocean that has been frozen for hundreds of millions of years. It's a long way from thinking about how trilobites learned about their new worlds. But when I first heard about complexity as a means for understanding, I felt an enormous sense of comfort, of being again in a position where I had once been, studying a new world through a new set of remote sensing tools. The tools are the computers we can now use to sift and recall incredible numbers of discrete transactions that are our culture's record of production and consumption of artifacts. John Holland writes in his book *Emergence* that finding order in chaos is a basic human urge. It is gratifying to reconnect my basic twenty-year-old dreams with a world where discovery matters, and where order can emerge from near-random chaos.

I can't help but wonder about whether this book can catalyze the development of a hit itself, and how that boom-or-bust phenomenon will play out. I hope that it conveys the sense of personal discovery and excitement I felt when discovering this new world. I hope that it helps managers and readers apply these ideas to their daily lives, just as it has to mine. Through this hit may we all become connected, and in that new network discover ourselves anew.

Once upon a time, a young man stepped onto the hard-packed surface of a sand dune that was three stories high. No human had been there for weeks beforehand. The sand was shaped by the predominant westerly wind, which had become quiet in the twilight. The young man took further steps onto the hard surface, where the countless number of interlocking quartz crystals formed a firm bedrock. As the light grew dimmer, his steps became less sure, now only guided by starlight before the moonrise. He recalled how important the moon had been to his education, and how the pattern of the craters on the moon had formed faces for some cultures, and scientific laboratories for others. He remembered the photograph of the far side of the moon, the one not normally visible from the earth's surface, that hung in James Adams's office at Stanford University.

Dr. Adams told of the importance of this viewpoint, which clearly showed a dark inner circle surrounded by two outer rings: prominent scars on the moon's surface, and nearly large enough to encompass the diameter of the moon. If that asteroid impact basin that formed that huge and prominent scar had been just five hundred miles to the east, it would have been seen from the earth. A chance impact had made it invisible to all except orbiting spacecraft. If it had been visible, however, it could have looked to some on earth like a god's eye staring down at us from on high. The man wondered what that would have done to mankind's development of religious beliefs and rituals.

Not paying attention, the man took a step and suddenly his foot sank far into a soft layer of sand, right up to his hip. In an instant an entire slipface of tons of sand started to slip down a sixty-foot escarpment. But more magical was the emergence of a growing sound—a steady deep bass tone of the sand as it moved. The vibration was making the earth literally move in a persistent standing wave, soon enveloping the entire dune. Across an expanse of two hundred yards, the dune's whole face was sliding—the noise became deafening, full of rich overtones and harmonics. The booming dune echoed across the desert, ricocheting sound off distant mountains, and causing other nearby dunes to respond in vibrational sympathy. After a few minutes, the dune's slipface slowed to a crawl, the sound fell to a whisper, and the young man sat and watched the moon rise over the low hills, knowing that the eye of God was looking the other way.

EPILOGUE

I'm pleased that this paperback edition of *How Hits Happen* gives me a chance to respond to readers who have asked for simple takeaways to apply to their business. While I can't guarantee anyone a hit—indeed, this book proves that hits cannot be manufactured—here are some simple steps that may help you surf the market.

1. *Open big.* Make an opening, an event; think of event films and niche films. Both are monopolies of the mind at a point in time. You know that you have successfully created a monopoly of the mind when the opening is like the last moments of the countdown. Across scattered groups of people, the anticipation builds up to the product's release, leading to a publicly celebrated launch. Think of the anticipation among both kids and their parents for the newest Harry Potter book, or the buzz around new summer movies.

2. *Find and nourish small worlds.* Recognize the loudmouths who can reinforce the message, and know how well they are connected. It's not a random world, remember. It's who you know that are in the know. That's why smart companies are hiring "cool hunters" to get an early lead on how products are taking off. Think beyond simply practicing one-to-one marketing:

look for opportunities to actually create networks of like-minded consumers to spread the word.

3. *Appeal to braggarts.* This means matching people's lifestyles with products, rather than submitting the product to fit the personality. The double-caf soy milk latte in the Starbucks cup makes a clear statement by a person who defines herself with this particular blend, and not just another cup of joe.

4. *Be different, but not too different.* If you are too similar to existing products or brands, then uniformity sets in. Tactics, logos, or products that are too easy to replicate invite a me-too erosion of the brand. Yet those that are too different—the weird outcast who steps in alone—prevent any meaningful conversation catalysis. Brand extensions, such as those by Crest, or Diet Coke from Coca-Cola, enable the crowd to both keep the trust and have something new to talk about.

5. *Get the positive buzz out.* Salt chat room conversations with enthusiastic reviews. Start chat rooms for fans. While too much hype may foster a negative response, it's important to try to seed conversation through tactics such as posting news articles on provocative sites or placing enticing teasers in surprising places.

6. *Give 'em prizes to take home.* T-shirts, for instance, matter. Many successful high-tech companies realize the talismanic value of creating a cool T-shirt (there's an entire museum of T-shirts from famous Silicon Valley companies as testament to their passion value). And what family member doesn't know how successfully Disney has spawned interest and further profits from their feature films from merchandising tie-ins?

7. *Look for "daylight" to run in.* Launch in the slow news day, the out-of-cycle month, the unusual and unexpected nonholi-

day promotion. The gamesmanship that studio executives practice in deciding when to open films applies equally to any manager launching a consumer product.

8. *Experiment and learn.* Explore the margins, not just a single monolithic marketing approach everywhere. Products like Dryel from Procter & Gamble and Go-Gurt, the portable yogurt from General Mills' Yoplait are results of experimental forays into new trails off well-trod paths.

9. *Build simultaneous multiple strategies.* One is too few, seven too many. Think of our products as a portfolio of potential hits, any of which could break out. Be prepared to react quickly to any one scenario rather than selecting one strategy ahead of time.

10. *Get out.* One day it will be clear that the downdraft is part of the downward trend. Produce what is needed, without inventory overhang, and move on. Just as theater owners quickly move their films from large theaters to smaller ones to make room for the next blockbuster, so too should you be ready to replace your hits with the next big thing.

BIBLIOGRAPHY

Arthur, W. Brian. *Increasing Returns and Path Dependence in the Economy*. Ann Arbor: University of Michigan Press, 1994.
This book pulls together Brian Arthur's most important papers on the subject of increasing returns. They are virtually the same versions that were published in academic journals and therefore range in mathematical and technical knowledge from virtually none to highly sophisticated. All the papers deal with increasing returns, but their subjects vary widely, from mathematical theorems to how industry locates in an urban area. Using both simulation and rigorous mathematics, Arthur convinces the reader that increasing returns is a vitally important subject, discussion of which will be more prevalent in the future.

Brandenburger, Adam, and Barry Nalebuff. *Co-opetition*. New York: Currency, 1996.
One of the first popular books to introduce game theory to managers, *Co-opetition* provides a surprisingly rich blend of theory and practical advice. The authors' strongest asset is their ability to illustrate game theory through a wide array of industries and examples and to explain how to view competition through an altogether different lens.

Capra, Fritjof. *The Web of Life: A New Scientific Understanding of Living Systems*. New York: Anchor Books, 1997.
Capra is an eclectic writer with an ambitious intellectual goal: to find the links between philosophical, scientific, and social thought systems. In this book he masterfully weaves together the foundations of complexity theory, systems thinking, self-organization, modern biology, and more, to show how these discoveries can allow us to rethink literally our place on the earth.

Epstein, Joshua M., and Robert Axtell. *Growing Artificial Societies: Social Science from the Bottom Up*. Cambridge, Mass.: Brookings Institution Press and MIT Press, 1995.
Although this book's dense language and scientific tenor may prove daunting for beginners, it's worth it. Epstein and Axtell provide a short but trenchant introduction arguing that computer simulations offer a chance to study social science by, in essence, growing societies and their dynamics. Then they demonstrate, in great detail, how such social phenomena as friendship and trade "emerge" from the interaction of individual agents following simple rules.

Gelertner, David Hillel. *Mirror Worlds, or The Day Software Puts the Universe in a Shoebox . . . How It Will Happen and What It Will Mean*. New York: Oxford University Press, 1991.
By envisioning the networked world as it could be, Gelertner describes computers as lenses that we can use to make sense of our world. Predating the Internet, this book depicts an imminent giant leap in technological capability. It contains fascinat-

ing accounts of artificial world models that are now being constructed and how these microcosms can help us better run hospitals, governments, and other real-world systems.

Gell-Mann, Murray. *The Quark and the Jaguar: Adventures in the Simple and the Complex*. New York: W. H. Freeman, 1994.
Gell-Mann is a Nobel laureate in physics who takes the reader on a journey from the simplest thing in the universe, the quark (a building block for the atom), to one of the most complex, the jaguar. Along the way, he touches on physics, math, and biology. Notable are the later chapters on sustainability, the environment, and public policy. The book's discussions on complexity in the physical world are outstanding—and not only show how the world is a complex adaptive system but suggest how it can be managed.

Hofstadter, Douglas R. *Gödel, Escher, Bach: An Eternal Golden Braid*. New York: Basic Books, 1979.
This is a marvelous book that weaves together math, art, and music into an unbreakable thread. Written almost two decades ago, it celebrates creativity without being pretentious. Once you have read it, your worldview will be forever altered. Those who read it a while ago should review it for further reinforcement. The book contains a series of dialogues between fictional characters that serve as preludes to chapters full of self-referential puns, puzzles, and precious gems of genius. Even though it predates the emergence of complexity theory, its connections are unmistakable. Note that it also won the 1980 Pulitzer prize for nonfiction.

Holland, John H. *Hidden Order: How Adaptation Builds Complexity.*
New York: Addison-Wesley, 1995.
Holland's book, which grew out of a series of lectures, gives a
concise yet thorough explanation of the nuts and bolts of
emergent behavior. Very much grounded in the mechanics of
how the theory works, this book manages to avoid much of the
hard-core mathematics and formulae of other scientific treat-
ments. Engaging and robust, this book serves as a wonderful
complement to Waldrop's *Complexity*, providing a rich scientific
background for the lay reader. For a look at finer details of Holland's views on complexity, try his *Emergence: From Chaos to Order*
(Addison-Wesley, 1998).

Kauffman, Stuart. *The Origins of Order: Self-Organization and Selection in Evolution.* New York: Oxford University Press, 1993.
An imposing book full of diagrams and tables that are themselves on the edge of chaos, Kauffman's first attempt to record
his life's work is still more content-rich than his more approach-
able *At Home in the Universe.* The treatment of self-organization in
biology and in economies is worth wading through the tough
mathematical sections; skipping passages that are not on-
point is one strategy that can mine the golden nuggets in this
rough ore.

Langton, Christopher G.; Charles Taylor; J. Doyne Farmer;
and Steen Rasmussen, eds. *Artificial Life II: Proceedings of the Santa
Fe Institute Studies in the Sciences of Complexity*, vol. 10. New York:
Addison-Wesley, 1992.
I have chosen this one volume to represent the number of solid
proceedings available in this continuing series of papers and

dialogues from the Santa Fe Institute. This particular volume dwells on the importance of artificial life and the stunning value of evolutionary programming of computers that can build "living" things.

Penrose, Roger. *Shadows of the Mind: A Search for the Missing Science of Consciousness.* New York: Oxford University Press, 1994.
Penrose takes us on a journey into the workings of the human mind and our paradoxical understanding of the world around us. Penrose's enormous intellect, backed by compelling and sometimes humorous visual sketches of the variety of mathematical models that demonstrate how complicated the world really is, leads to truly compelling stories and arguments about our underlying inability to understand our own consciousness.

Resnick, Mitchell. *Turtles, Termites, and Traffic Jams: Explorations in Massively Parallel Microworlds.* Cambridge, Mass.: MIT Press, 1994.
Resnick, a former journalist who is now an assistant professor in the media laboratory at MIT, has written a passionate book that explores how the lessons gleaned from complexity and computer simulations can literally change how people think and learn. Resnick explains the limitations of the "centralized mind-set" in everything from markets to governments to consciousness. He then explores in detail how the modeling exercises made possible by Starlogo, a computer programming language, can help people learn from the ground up, through construction and design, as opposed to simple instruction. Resnick is particularly interested in probing how these issues can affect education. In the final chapters, he reflects on how

changing their mind-set from a centralized to a decentralized one enables people to see the world more clearly.

Senge, Peter M. *The Fifth Discipline: The Art and Practice of the Learning Organization*. New York: Currency, 1990.
Although many believe the promise of this book is to teach "the art and practice of the learning organization," its hidden asset is a friendly explanation of systems thinking—which, in Senge's model, represents the "fifth discipline" necessary for organizational learning (along with personal mastery, mental models, shared vision, and team learning). For Senge, systems thinking is about "seeing patterns where others see only events and forces to react to" and about "organizing complexity into a coherent story that illuminates the causes of problems and how they can be remedied in enduring ways." Although Senge may not always provide strong data for the stories he presents, he nonetheless explains how, in a large system, myriad agents and dynamics can be ultimately connected to one another. And his ideas for using systems thinking to produce change both individually and in groups are quite compelling.

Waldrop, M. Mitchell. *Complexity: The Emerging Science at the Edge of Order and Chaos*. New York: Touchstone, 1992.
This book is an excellent starting point for learning the basics of complexity. In telling the story of how an eclectic group of scientists came together to create the Santa Fe Institute, Waldrop presents this subject more as scientific thriller than textbook. He shows how the thinking and personalities of the

various pioneers evolved into the school of thought now called complexity. Moreover, he writes in a clear and vivid style that serves the material even in its most complicated arenas. Above all, Waldrop's book provides relevance by showing how and where this growing school of thought applies to our lives.

INDEX